WRITING SELVES

WRITING SELVES

Contemporary Feminist Autography

JEANNE PERREAULT

University of Minnesota Press

Minneapolis

London

Portions of chapter 1 first appeared as " 'that the pain not be wasted': Audre Lorde and the Written Self," *a/b: auto/biography studies* 4 (Fall 1988): 1–16, by permission; chapter 3 first appeared as "Refracting Selves: Kate Millett's *The Basement*," reprinted by permission from the 14th issue, number 2, of *Prose Studies*, published by Frank Cass & Company, 890/900 Eastern Avenue, Ilford, Essex, England, copyright Frank Cass & Co., Ltd.; selected lines from "North American Time," "Sources," and "Contradictions: Tracking Poems" are reprinted from *Your Native Land, Your Life: Poems by Adrienne Rich,* by permission of the author and W. W. Norton & Company, Inc., copyright 1986 by Adrienne Rich; "Delta" is reprinted from *Time's Power: Poems 1985–1988,* by Adrienne Rich, by permission of the author and W. W. Norton & Company, Inc., copyright 1989 by Adrienne Rich.

Published by the University of Minnesota Press
111 Third Avenue South, Suite 290, Minneapolis, MN 55401-2520
Printed in the United States of America on acid-free paper

Library of Congress Cataloging-in-Publication Data
Perreault, Jeanne Martha.
Writing selves : contemporary feminist autography / Jeanne Perreault.
p.   cm.
Includes bibliographical references and index.
ISBN 0-8166-2654-5 (alk. paper). — ISBN 0-8166-2655-3 (pbk. : alk. paper)
1. American literature — Women authors — History and criticism.
2. Feminism and literature — United States — History — 20th century.
3. Women and literature — United States — History — 20th century.
4. American literature — 20th century — History and criticism.
5. Women — United States — Biography — History and criticism.   6. Rich, Adrienne Cecile — Criticism and interpretation.   7. Williams, Patricia J., 1951–   Alchemy of race and rights.   8. Lorde, Audre. Cancer journals.   9. Millett, Kate. Basement.   10. Self in literature.   11. Autobiography.   I. Title.
PS151.P47   1995   95-8529

To my daughter, Jennifer Elsa Perreault, and her son
Jordan Joseph Perreault
born November 12, 1994

Contents

~

Acknowledgments

This volume owes much to the suggestions that Amy Kaminsky, Verena Andermatt Conley, and, especially, Rebecca Hogan made in their readers' reports for the University of Minnesota Press. I am happy to thank them and Biodun Iginla. I gratefully acknowledge Adrienne Rich and Norton Publishers, Frank Cass Co. Ltd., and *a/b: auto/biography studies* for permission to use material.

I have elected, in this volume, not to produce (explicitly) my own autography. I do wish, however, to foreground one personal fact. I am a Canadian, not an American, and as an outsider, albeit one who lived in the United States in the early empassioned days of the women's liberation movement, I wish to thank the women I met there so long ago who gave me much to bring home, the possibilities of feminist energy and ongoing transformations that charged some of that border crossing with passion and hope. The American writers I discuss continue to move me deeply with their power of mind, their sustained commitment to the worlds they are in, and their generosity of words and selves. I thank them, especially Audre Lorde, who died while this book was in progress. Her death grieves all women who know her work, and *The Cancer Journals* continues to bring strength as women pass it from hand to hand.

To the individuals who have made life, as well as this book, seem possible I am pleased to offer the following thanks.

Loving thanks go to Shirley Neuman, most generous feminist scholar, teacher, friend, and hiker extraordinaire. To Patricia Clements, who was there at the beginning, making a passionate intellectual life seem possible, and who is still there, my thanks, always. Thank you to my old friends who have been hearing about this project for so long, who have helped make life worth living while I sought and resisted completion, who read bits (or wholes) and gave excellent advice and enabling support: Maureen Malloy, Susan Westren, Anne Scholefield, Sylvia Vance, Joanna Dunbar, and George Samuel. I gratefully acknowledge my debt to Cheryl Malmo and Janet Wright for letting writing happen. I acknowledge with appreciation the encouragement in crucial moments of Brad Bucknell and Ashraf Rushdy.

My friends at the University of Calgary have been exemplary, and I owe them much for making a context in which feminist antiracist scholarship can breathe. In particular I want to thank Cherry Bowhay, Aritha van Herk, Mavis Reimer, and Fred Wah. Special and very warm thanks must go to those friends who so willingly have read sections of the final draft, bringing their fierce readerly eyes and generous spirits to the writing, and the pleasure of their company to the writer: Pauline Butling, Susan Bennett, and Susan Rudy Dorscht.

I wish my father, Joseph Leopold Cyrlle Perreault, had lived to see this book appear. He wanted to hear my "women's stories" to the end of his very long life, and he would have loved the drama of publication.

To thank my mother, Elsie Perreault, for her support in every way through the tangled years, for her sustaining love, and for her trust in learning seems not enough. But I do thank her.

Much has been said about how parents shape children, but little of how a child shapes a mother. I here wish to acknowledge the shaping power of my daughter, Jennifer Elsa Perreault, on my life, and to thank her.

CHAPTER ONE

Autography/Transformation/ Asymmetry

> In the fact that the subject is a *process* lies the
> possibility of transformation.
> CATHERINE BELSEY, "Constructing the Subject:
> Deconstructing the Text"

> For silence to transform into speech, sounds and words, it must first
> traverse through our female bodies.
> GLORIA ANZALDÚA, *Making Face, Making Soul*

"I" and "we" are the most important words in the writing(s) of contemporary feminism, continuously transformed and reenacted as feminists claim the rights of self-definition. This process of transformation, these texts, works actively and explicitly in the context of feminist communities, communities that are, I will argue, inextricable from discourses of selfhood. Throughout this study, textual enactments of an "I" and the boundaries of "we" are in play as elements of inquiry, as territories to be claimed and disclaimed, as constructions or as essences. Feminist writers of all races, sexualities, and classes interrogate discourses of power, identity, and experience as alternative

discourses become available through the speaking of greater numbers of women.[1] The feminist texts effected by this process of self
writing make the female body of she who says "I" a site and source of
written subjectivity, investing that individual body with the shifting
ethics of a political, racial, and sexual consciousness. These intersecting layers of mediation inform feminist autography. One of my aims
is to explore in the writing of self how the continual revision of these
categories (self/community/identity) is central to the way in which
feminism makes itself continuously meaningful.

In referring to the texts of significant contemporary feminist writers as "autographies," I am naming a kind of writing that can and
should be identified in order to foreground the suggestive and flexible processes of both *autos* and *graphia*. Much contemporary self
writing does not fall within the parameters of familiar modes of "I"
writing (autobiography, life writing, memoirs, etc.), and various feminist theorists and critics have been grappling with unwieldy generic
terminology that does not seem to fit women's texts. Here, I read
Audre Lorde, Adrienne Rich, Kate Millett, Patricia Williams, and others, looking to textual configurations of a subjectivity precisely articulated in the varied forms that I call "autography."[2] In autography, I
find a writing whose effect is to bring into being a "self" that the
writer names "I," but whose parameters and boundaries resist the
monadic. Writing "I" has been an emancipatory project for women,
and a crucial one in the evolution of contemporary American[3] feminism. This study addresses who and what is meant by that written
"I" as an element in the "we" of feminist communities, and takes up
problems of feminist articulations of self and writing in the context
of current debates of subjectivity. Although I rehearse some of the
arguments of contemporary theorists, my focus is on the texts that
explicitly make the process of being a self contiguous with the inscription of selfhood. The forms I examine here, including poems,
"meditations," and journals, share some common ground: each writer
names herself "I" and "feminist," and reveals that the process of self-
in-the-making is made available to the reader. Autography, then, as I
conceive it, invites the reader to reconsider the imbrications of subjectivity, textuality, and community.

The American feminist exists in a context of intense, almost obsessive, ideology of attention to "the individual." She is informed by a passion for social justice and a will toward discerning how that might be enacted. Recent discussions of multiplicity of "selves," or the deconstruction of the figure of the indivisible "self," have not so much undermined the valorizing of selfhood as extended it, giving the "selves" a share in the belief in the rights of the individual. These perspectives underlie the struggle to find a "voice," a place from which to speak, and the continual revising of feminist discourses is the most secure of feminism's practices. It is in the mutable, capacious space and time of the written (that is, the public, published) text that feminist discourses of selfhood, "freedom," and ethics, recombine under, or through, the sign of "I." My readings of what I am calling autography look to writers whose feminism is embodied, historically precise, self-reflective, and communally shaped: Audre Lorde's *The Cancer Journals*; the later prose and poetry of Adrienne Rich; Kate Millett's *The Basement: Meditations on a Human Sacrifice*; and Patricia Williams's *The Alchemy of Race and Rights: diary of a law professor.* Even if we think that feminism may be about many other things than the subjectivity of the feminist,[4] the importance of this "subject" in feminist discourse can hardly be overestimated, and it is her varied voice that we find in feminist autography. Throughout this study I demonstrate how each writer traces the discursive boundaries of her identity, and illustrate the impossibility of imposing a metadiscourse on the texts of feminist subjectivity.

Categories and Communities

Feminist theorists of autobiography and life writing have been grappling with modes of expression that evade the familiar narrative of life events. Simultaneously, and not coincidentally, discussions of "identity" and subjectivity, and ongoing reconsiderations of categories of "women" and "feminism" push literary and feminist theory in new directions. One way in which autography differs from autobiography is that it is not necessarily concerned with the process or unfolding of life events, but rather makes the writing itself an aspect of the selfhood the writer experiences and brings into being. In their generically unfixed literary productions, contemporary feminist autographers have been enacting subjectivity in multiple and various ways. These writers make "I" and "we" signify both continuity with an ongoing life in a body and a community, and dissociation within that life — gaps, amputations, silences. That self-in-the-making defies, and affirms, some of the most provocative aspects of contemporary theory and reinforces the tentative proposals of feminist theorists that a new kind of subjectivity is evolving.

The texts produced by this process simultaneously reshape female subjectivity and agency while reinscribing the possibility, experience, and value of being a "self." The problematics of these concepts — subjectivity, agency, self — form the basis of a writing of self whose parameters are relentlessly mobile. The woman who speaks "I" in feminist autography seems to have anticipated the procedure that Denise Riley suggests for theorists: "Instead of veering between deconstruction and transcendence, we could try another train of speculations: that 'women' is indeed an unstable category, . . . that feminism is the site of the systematic fighting-out of that instability" (Riley, "Am I That Name?" 5). Riley is addressing the issue from the perspective of those talking *about* women. My concern, however, is the voice of she who writes in the body of a woman, when "I" and "woman" (the singular of "women," not the blank screen of historical specularities and speculations) are embraced as unstable categories, territories to be inhabited, claimed, or reclaimed — not colonized, but worked and revised. Tania Modleski speaks of "a way to hold on to the category of woman while recognizing ourselves to be in the *process* (an unending one) of *defining and constructing the category*" (Modleski, *Feminism without Women* 20). A category in process does not cease to be a category.[5]

The central questions for feminists are these: Who will construct the categories into which "I" and "we" fit ourselves? Whose words will we attend to? Whose texts will we honor? Audre Lorde declares, "If we don't name ourselves we are nothing" ("Interview" 19). Here, Lorde predicates being upon naming: those who are named by others have no way to exist in and for themselves. Yet the "we" is somehow in existence, known to itself, available for the naming. Audre Lorde frames a "we" that situates her clearly among those who are vulnerable to being named from the outside and thus, paradoxically, created for others' purposes while being eliminated for their own. Lorde's assertion addresses one of the ongoing sites of negotiation in the making of a movement. The processes that the texts of self-writing enact are not solitary or sovereign, and any discussion of a feminist "I" must take into account the register of "we," a contested zone that resists definition but asserts its own existence. Cherríe Moraga says:

> Our strategy is how we cope — how we measure and weigh what is to be said and when, what is to be done and how, and to whom and to whom and to whom, daily deciding/risking who it is we can call an ally, call a friend (whatever that person's skin, sex, or sexuality). We are women without a line. We are women who contradict each other. (Moraga and Anzaldúa, *This Bridge Called My Back* xix)

Here Moraga, as a woman of color speaking with other women of color, asserts the identity that ensues as lives are enmeshed with those of others for self-defense and social transformation. Allies and friends are not assumed, but decided upon; and the decision is made daily, provisionally. To be "women without a line" is to eschew a correct line, to see borderlines as mobile, and to take responsibility for coping. Strategy is no abstraction. Moreover, contradiction does not destroy "we-ness" in Moraga's view; rather, it is necessarily part of a subjectivity that is discursive *and* embodied. The subject Moraga configures (here, both agent and topic) anticipates what Teresa de Lauretis calls a "feminist concept of identity." This is de Lauretis's definition: "a political-personal strategy of survival and resistance that is also, at the same time, a critical practice and a mode of knowledge" ("Issues, Terms, and Contexts" 9). Both de Lauretis and Moraga use the word "strategy," thereby asserting identity as purposeful, intentional practice, and a "mode of knowledge," a "daily deciding" that is necessarily provisional, modifying action and being modified in a dialectic of everydayness.[6] As these definitions suggest,

identity is valued as mobile and transformational, communal as well
as private.

This problematic of subjectivity is complexly implicated in an identity politics that must confront the issues of representation when to
"represent" means to speak for, to speak about, and, most troublingly,
to speak as. "Identity politics" as a politically effective principle was
first explicitly articulated in "The Combahee River Collective Statement" when socialist Black lesbian feminists asserted the specificity
of their experience and oppression as the basis of their political organizing. The Collective reports that Black women describe "feelings of craziness" until concepts allowing group identification are
available (211). The "seemingly personal experiences" of sexist or racist
abuses can be reframed as political when the "concepts of sexual politics [and] ... racial politics" come together in antiracist, feminist practice and analysis (211–12). The issues, problems, and possibilities that
arise in these assertions invite speculation about the intersection of
experiences and discourses within the person. She who is feeling
crazy is certainly (whatever else) feeling dislocated from her world.
The discourse communities of which she is a part are inadequate to
her "feeling" or "experience." It is this gap between the conceptual
and the experiential that feminist self-writers (and theorists) explore
as the zone most available for modification.

The forms of feminist autography are widely varied, generically
unbounded, modifying ways of seeing the world and being selves in
it. As available discourses of selfhood have been largely masculinist,
the sense of self that the feminist writer has at any moment must be
a mixture of contradictory and shifting configurations of personhood, and her interpretation of those configurations will inevitably
refigure both them and her "self." When "self" is written (whether that
is understood to mean described, [re]presented, [re]created, articulated, or fixed), the distinction between the received models of selfhood and the "autobiographical impulse to self invention" can again
be brought into play, to be revised, necessarily, in the next sentence
(Eakin, *Fictions* 6). Paul Eakin looks to the "dialectical interplay between the autobiographical impulse to self-invention and received

models of selfhood" (6), but he does not examine the degree to which
a Western cultural imperative toward "selfhood" may *include* "self-
invention." When "received models" of self are narrow and too uniform, self-invention may be an imperative.

The will toward self-making, in feminist textual practice, is mul-
tidimensional. Autography asserts a highly indeterminate feminism
and an equally indeterminate notion of selfhood. As women write
themselves, categories of difference (inner, outer, body, world, language) do not disappear, but take shape as "I" and in relation to "I."
The shifts in relations between personal, body-specific identity and
communal, or ideological, identity (the I who says we) both maintain
ongoingness and require discontinuity. To the extent that "I" and "we"
are imbricated in feminist autography, tracing the modulations of
representation is the crux of feminist thought. The texts that are effected anticipate and extend the problematic of subjectivity. The feminist "self," then, exists in the particulars of feminist texts and not in
any particular kind of text. Like all writing, feminist self-writing is
informed by the experiences of the everyday, of the body, of the sites
of contact with and isolation from the read-about and lived-in worlds.
But that world as the writer lives it can be imagined, felt, and recognized only from the writing.

Most often in feminist texts the "self" is provisional, an exploration
of possibility and a tentative grammar of transformations. Rather than
treating "self" as a fixed notion, clearly conceptualized and needing
only to be "expressed," the feminist writer of self engages in a (community of) discourse of which she is both product and producer.
This interrelation of self and community is one of the most provocative issues in the writing of feminist subjectivity. Political or ideological consciousness takes into account the intersections of individual
experience in its complexities of race, sexuality, class, ethnicity. The
feminist writing of self, then, is part of creating new communities.
Jane Marcus observes in women's self-writing a "structure that insists on the reader's response and sets the writer in conversation with
her own community" and suggests that this will toward the discursive is the moving spirit of women's autobiography (141). Once again:

as women write themselves they write the movement. The transformations of self, of community, and of material reality are brought to
possibility and registered in the writing.

Self/self?

The crisis in representation for feminist *and* masculinist theorists is
founded largely upon the relation of subjectivity to language. Jacques
Lacan's essentializing descriptions of the processes by which human
beings enter a uniform human community of language, and modernity's enthusiastic dislocation of words from things, have been in-
terestingly messed up by feminist theorists. Some, like Susan Friedman, have little patience with those issues. Friedman notes that in
much women's autobiography self is not "a false image of alienation,
an empty play of words on the page disconnected from the realm of
referentiality" ("Women's Autobiographical Selves" 40). Alienation,
she says, "is not the result of creating a self in language," but instead
it is "alienation from the historically imposed image of the self" that
"motivates the writing" (41).

   Outlining the deconstructions of the "humanist self" (105) and
the authority of representation it rests upon, Alice Jardine turns her
feminist light on those valorizations of fragmentation and alienation
that characterize the deconstructed self and the undermined possibility of representation. She observes the obsessive[7] "voiding" of the
person and looks warily at the complacency of "man's seemingly hope-
less alienation from his 'self' " (Jardine, *Gynesis* 106) attributed to the
foreign language of his unconscious: the "mother tongue."[8] Jardine
suggests that the feminist critic must be sensitive to the creation of
and cutting up of the maternal voice as (possibly) at the heart (ear)
of these "positivities of alienation" (116–17). The feminist critic must
conclude that the male writers of modernity or deconstruction rely
on their fantasies, wishes, or fears of the "feminine" to "subvert the
Subject, Representation, and Truth" (168–69). The construction of
the "feminine" has little if anything to do with women as subjects or
agents of language. De Lauretis observes that woman serves as "the
empty space between the signs" (*Alice* 8). Multiple subjectivities and

enabled agency have little kinship with that alienated, tragically and eternally divided-from-itself self of much psychoanalytic theory.[9]

To speak at all as subjects is to resist "the feminine"; that is, for women to speak as subjects subverts the view that it is the *idea* of the "feminine" that subverts male surfaces. In contrast to the sense of self put forward by Roland Barthes, for example, in which fragmentation is not only inevitable but desirable (*Roland Barthes* 93–94), Nancy K. Miller observes that women "have not felt burdened by too much Self, Ego, and Cogito, etc.," and thus have less investment in the fragmentation of identity ("Changing" 106). Jardine, Miller, de Lauretis, and others defy the necessary alienation of self from self, proposing a female subject that is not bound (or boundaried) by the masculinist discourse on subjectivity.

Some versions of this female speaking subject lie uneasily alongside one another. Two differently rooted, but oddly similar, modes of discourse affirm female selfhood, claiming the right to "voice" and the space to resist as simultaneous gestures. The excesses of High Feminist Selfhood, which I call the rhetoric of Self, share certain sisterly qualities with the ecstasies of *écriture feminine*.

A direct defiance of the specific authorities of psychoanalytic theory appears in *écriture feminine,* or writing "in the feminine."[10] This complicated form of literary expression is not necessarily writing by women, but is the articulation of the inarticulable "Other." As a psychoanalytic construct, the "Other" is that which is not the (conscious) self. Variously thought of as the unconscious (Freud), the denied (Irigaray), the repressed (Lacan), the presymbolic, or prelinguistic (Kristeva), it has gained extraordinary currency as a metaphor for whatever appears to disrupt a uniform presence, authority, or (re)presentation.[11] As it is thought to live in the preverbal zone, *écriture feminine* is often spoken of as "writing the body." Privileging the biological as female territory, Hélène Cixous says, "Women must write through their bodies" ("Medusa" 256). She breaks the grip of (male) reason on writing, insisting that "women are body. More body, hence more writing" (257). The reassertion of the connection between female body and "feminine" text makes writing "in the feminine" particularly complicated given the metaphoric function of "Woman."

The analogy of "excess" (that is, beyond usefulness to male purposes) is relied on here. The female body is fetishized in its site of specific orgasmic pleasure (*jouissance*) and excess comes to be representative of all expression of female pleasure, all feminine writing.[12] Whether or not these requirements for ecstatic expression meet all women's needs, Cixous's reclamation of the link between writing and voice is highly suggestive. It asserts the primacy of the lived-in body as the locus of language. Her well-known description of the violent distress of the woman speaking ("She doesn't 'speak,' she throws her trembling body in the air, she lets herself go" [*Newly Born* 93]) is of particular interest for the issue of female subjectivity and for women's self-writing. Cixous makes the link that deconstructive theorists (for example, Derrida or Barthes) deny has validity — of "*writing and voice*" (*Newly Born* 92). This connection is a complex one — and in the context of contemporary theory, the desire to dislocate writing from "voice" has become the dismantling of "phallogocentrism." Voice means presence, presence means origin, and origin implies Logos/the Word, the Godhead, the authority of Truth — the source and substance of power. That the maternal, the mother's body, is never considered as "source" or as "origin" suggests a certain resistance to embodiment as presence.[13] What Cixous's "privilege of *voice*" (92) exposes is that the practice of writing takes women to self, to body, to presence, and rejects the "transcendental anonymity" of writing/language detached from the context of its production.[14] Only if "voice" or "presence" is assumed to be that of the most profound of authorities, indeed, a voice or presence not limited by social or political conditions, is it necessary to detach it from writing.[15] And if we mean by female writing "subject" a complex, multiple, mutable (and self-consciously so) voice — a self for whom authorial "sovereignty" is not only a foreign image, but also a distasteful one, then that subject exists, and not in solitude.

Because the female body has so often been the object of male discourse, *écriture feminine* has the great appeal of seeming to be the voice of the female body speaking itself as subject. The delight of flaunting bodies so long un/covered in men's-only scripts is intense. But despite the pleasure for the writer or the reader, and it is full of that, *écriture feminine* cannot provide a sufficiently complex approach to the question of the written self in a feminist context. The erasure or negation of differences among women is a serious weakness of *écriture feminine*, as it is of the Rhetoric of Selfhood discourse. The female body and, indeed, whole being (in abstraction) is, once again, reconstructed as an absolute, defined by women, yes, but women who appear to have taken on the habits of mind of universalizing female experience.[16] To write "the body," as Adrienne Rich notes, is, once more, to take women out of history, economics, class, race—that is, out of either the specific and particular experience of self or the discourse of the surrounding culture (*Blood* 215).[17]

Like *écriture feminine*, the text of the rhetoric of feminist selfhood is often celebratory, affirmative, and exhortatory, influential as source and substance of feminist energy. Here is one of the best examples of it:

> Feminists are positing an original, wild, radical wholeness in the Self which is constantly unfolding. This whole self has certainly been subjected to violent, oppressive, forced splitting ... we seek to heal the splits and dismemberments of patriarchy through our intuition of an original wholeness.... Feminism is the articulated urge to lay claim to a larger, active, holistic view of ourSelves. It is at once our starting point and our goal ... the oppression [is not] the primary constitution of a woman's Self. Indeed, the oppressive conditions are a shock, a weight, a drain, precisely because they are a shock to something, a weight on something, a drain of something. That something is a sense of integrity of Self, a Self that may only or mostly exist as potential.... Radical feminism speaks to the deep Self in women. (Culpepper, "Simone" 11–12)

This abstracted, generalized, universalized (but not essentialized—it may exist only as "potential"), capital "S" Self is rhetoricized as primary presence and rightful goal, as precious possession and object of desire. The "something" that registers oppression as felt experience or "sense of integrity" preexists oppression's shocks, weights, or violations.[18] Not the least of the rhetoricized Self's potentialities is that it can be rearticulated as "subject" whose aim is to heal the "Self-splitting" (Daly, *Gyn/Ecology* 18) imposed by the phallic model of development, which requires a hostile gap between the "preoedipal" and "oedipal" phases of relationship to the symbolic.

In this model's division of psyche into Self and Other, the feminine is necessarily Other and a female "self" from which to establish a subject position is anomalous. Feminist rhetoric of Self refuses and refutes Lacan's (hopeful?) declaration that "she [woman] does not correspond to a self-in-language."[19] It appropriates the discourse of the Other, rejecting the silence it offers to women.

While they are too general, too enthusiastic, and too unself-conscious of their underlying assumptions to constitute ongoing feminist theory, these ecstatic "wild" affirmations of presence, with the possibility of change and the value of each female self they imply, have been welcomed strongly by many feminists. And despite their limitations, both kinds of inspirational feminist writing bear a peculiar relationship to the writing of self that concerns me here. Their shared belief in the existence of a "self," undefined but capable of resistance, energizes the transformation of women into "new social subjects." The embrace of "original" cosmic energy that finds itself configured as a Great Mother or a Medusa, however, leaves many feminists frustrated, perhaps because another fixed place, another reification, has been established, leaving the material existence of, and thus differences among, women unexamined.

Ironically, or inevitably, one of the most influential antiessentialist arguments to enter feminist debate, Judith Butler's *Gender Trouble: Feminism and the Subversion of Identity* (1990), suffers from a parallel absence of consideration of embodied, historically specific female identities.[20] Butler's aim is to undo the "foundational illusion" of that traditional subject, and in the process enact a proliferation of genders that will expose the performative basis of gender and inevitably displace the very grounding of binary power structures. This assumption of the emancipatory nature of her project and the absence of a politics that takes on materiality are the central weaknesses for me in Butler's argument in *Gender Trouble*.[21] Multiplying gender performativity, denaturalizing sexual desire, and unfixing sexual self-presence can be effects only of a cultural field in which women, like men (or, indeed, like those who refuse either category), have a public voice with which to say "I" and "we." This may be the unspoken assumption behind her assertion that the "critical task for feminism" ... is "to affirm the local possibilities of intervention through participating in precisely those practices of repetition that constitute identity and, therefore, present the immanent possibility of contesting them" (147). When Butler concludes *Gender Trouble* with the declaration that "the deconstruction of identity is not the deconstruction of politics; rather, it establishes as political the very terms through which identity is articulated" (148), I have a peculiar sense of being informed that the personal is political. My recollection, however, is that it is feminism, rather than deconstruction, that "establishes as political the very terms through which identity is articulated."

    Gender Trouble bases its antiessentialist position on its refusal of a metaphysics of substance, and reasserts another metaphysics, one curiously consistent with the image of the "historically abstract and substantively empty subject" that Anthony Cascardi observes is necessary to hold together modernity's " 'detotalized' whole" (*Subject* 35). Butler participates in that "intellectual abstraction of the 'subject' from the real conditions of its existence," an approach that Paul Smith notes is "perfectly consonant" with a "western philosophical heritage in which the 'subject' is construed as the unified and coherent bearer of consciousness" (*Discerning* xxx). To fulfill the deconstructive project of "voiding" the unified and coherent subject (Jardine, *Gynesis* 106), while accounting for the possibility of social change, Butler, following Nietzsche, separates the idea of a "doer" from the deed, eliminating the doer altogether. Butler cites Nietzsche's declaration: "There is no 'being' behind doing, effecting, becoming; 'the doer' is merely a fiction added to the deed" (Butler, *Gender* 25).[22] Her own corollary to Nietzsche — "There is no gender identity behind the expressions of gender; that identity is performatively constituted by the very 'expressions' that are said to be its results" (*Gender* 25) — she follows with the assertion: "A great deal of feminist theory and literature has *nevertheless* assumed that there is a 'doer' behind the deed" (my emphasis, *Gender* 25). While Butler's "nevertheless" carries the surprising assumption that "feminist theory and literature" *should* be corrected by Nietzsche's signature, the more important issue is Butler's apparent conclusion that a "doer" is only *one* thing, presumably the singular, unified, sovereign subject of Western tradition. If it is not that, it cannot exist at all. Even the later, more complex, argument of *Bodies That Matter* resists the possibility of a dialectic between the speaker and the spoken "I": she says, "There is no 'I' who stands *behind* discourse and executes its volition or will *through* discourse. On the contrary, the 'I' only comes into being through being called, named, interpellated" (*Bodies* 225). It is the absolute authority of the external that most perplexes me in Butler's position. Much of her later discussion of subjectivity corrects *Gender Trouble*'s blind spots and clarifies her perspective, but this passivity remains. To caution against the "expectation of self-determination that self-naming arouses" (*Bodies* 228) and to alert the naive to the fiction that "self-naming" will "make oneself in and through the magic of the name" (228), free of historical residue, free of the chains of "prior usage," will make most sense in the context of naming oneself *something*. In Butler's discussion, however, resistance to the reifications attending identity politics, alongside the refutation of monadic self-creation, has foreclosed examination of an "I" that not only is not colonized by language, but that also is not made up wholly of language. Butler says, for example, "Recognition is not conferred on a subject, but forms that subject," and concludes, "the 'I' is thus a citation of the place of the 'I' in speech, where that place has a certain priority and anonymity with respect to the life it animates; it is the historically revisable possibility of a name that precedes and exceeds me, but without which I cannot speak" (*Bodies* 226). The weight here is on the substantiality (though always provisional) of the signifier, "a citation of the place of the 'I' in speech." The odd effect of this mode of representation of "I" is to place the speaker (the "I" embodied) as always already signified, cited, placed, animated, preceded, and exceeded. Self (a word that has no home in a Butlerian neighborhood), however complicated by multiplicities, could not be imagined to precede or exceed the discursive "I," nor could it exist in some fluidity of exchange or blurred boundary with the formative performativity conferred by language.

Various feminist theorists refuse the dichotomy required by the essentialist/antiessentialist paradigms. Diana Fuss tracks the path of "essence" through Lacanian psychoanalysis and Derridian deconstruction, asserting its inevitability as a crucial "hidden" element in those signposts of antiessentialist thought (*Essentially Speaking* 19). Fuss refuses to essentialize essentialism (21), and insists on the more complex position of assessing the political valence of essentialism based on "*who* is utilizing it, *how* it is deployed, and *where* its effects are concentrated" (20). Patricia Hill Collins eludes the grip of the dichotomy by placing "Black women's subjectivity in the center of [her] analysis" as "only one angle of vision" (*Black Feminist Thought* 234). By asserting the validity of both the "legitimacy of their knowledge claims" (232) and the partial and situated perspectives that are no less characteristic of Black feminist thought than any other, Collins sidesteps the fruitless argument of objective absolute truths or relativist homogenized equalization of differences (235). Elizabeth Spelman, like Collins, argues for a specifically situated consciousness that recognizes and takes responsibility for acknowledging the unspoken, the submerged markers of privilege that inform dominant discourses (*Inessential Woman* 176).

These theorists, like many others, rely on a notion of "situated knowledges" to discuss feminist positionality, and it is useful, I think, to recall that Donna Haraway's original assertion declares itself to be, in the context of a feminist science, "a doctrine of embodied objectivity" (*Simians* 188): "Feminist objectivity means quite simply *situated knowledges*" (188). "Easy relativisms and holisms," insists Haraway, will not do, nor will a merely "acknowledged and self-critical partiality" (192). Her assertion (which must be figured within a discourse of resistant science — refuting the "god-trick" of masculinist "objectivity") is so richly evocative that I will quote a rather long section from her remarks on the "Western eye" as a figure of perspective:

> The knowing self is partial in all its guises, never finished, whole, simply there and original; it is always constructed and stitched together imperfectly, and *therefore* able to join with another, to see together without claiming to be another. Here is the promise of objectivity: a scientific knower seeks the subject position not of identity, but of objectivity; that is, partial connection. (193)

In addition to the reminder that partiality is a necessary condition of connection, what is most interesting to me in this assertion is

Haraway's clear invocation of a "knowing self." Her argument draws the imperfections and raggedness, the stitchedness and constructedness of it; yet, it exists, and is active in seeking one subject position over another. In effect, agent and knowing self seek, construct, or select subject-positions that can be provisionally, partially inhabited from a standpoint of ethical subjectivity.

Feminist subjectivity and subject position overlap, but positionality, however significant an element it is, even in a provisional or mobile sense of the term cannot contain the subject. To enable my reading of feminist autographies, these categories and conceptions require delicate, flexible, and clear affiliations. And at the heart of the matter, the question of self beats. In *Thinking Fragments*, Jane Flax (1990) distinguishes between the concepts of a "unitary" or singular self and a "core" self. Flax observes that in postmodernist discourses on subjectivity, "all possible forms of self are confounded with the unitary, mentalist, deeroticised, masterful and oppositional selves they rightly criticize" (218). With some impatience, Flax suggests that those who "celebrate or call for a 'decentered' self seem self-deceptively naive and unaware of the basic cohesion within themselves that makes the fragmentation of experiences something other than a terrifying slide into psychosis" (218–19). Acknowledging that "fragmentation of experiences" is felt, lived, undergone as part of the sensation of personhood, Flax insists on the distinction between that sense of a multiplicity of "selves" and the shattering that takes place when no one within a body is able to say "I" and include all her "selves." The self Flax refers to may be the same self Elspeth Probyn describes: "The self has to be stretched but not broken, folded but not rendered schizophrenic. We need to manipulate and bend ourselves but this is not inward action conducted in the hallucinations of self-supremacy" (*Sexing the Self* 129). This "deep" malleable subjectivity (Flax 210) or cohesion is what I imagine Donna Haraway affirms in her statement that "the split and contradictory self is the *one* who can interrogate positionings and be accountable, the *one* who can construct and join rational conversation and fantastic imaginings that change history" (my emphasis, *Simians* 193). Haraway, here, emphasizes the splits and the contradictions within the conscious self, whereas my emphasis draws attention to the force of cohesion that seems to inhabit, to move among, and perhaps to make possible the various subject positions. That personal consciousness of continuity, even the kind of continuity that signals rupture, is a "going-on-being"ness that Flax asserts is "so much a part of the core self that it becomes a taken-for-granted background" (219).

As commodious as Flax's argument is, the figure of the "core" she relies on to articulate the nature of selfhood is distracting. It constricts response by inviting the polarity of centers and margins, and reifying the "I" in a fixed metaphor of location. I believe Flax's term can be read as "energy" rather than as "object" or "location." This energy, then, manifesting itself textually as "I," has the power to bracket, elide, connect, or differentiate parts of self and world. Here is Flax's description of that core self in action: "Only when a core self begins to cohere can one enter into or use the transitional space in which the differences and boundaries between self and other, inner and outer, and reality and illusion are bracketed or elided" (219). Not only does Flax insist on its existence, but she claims that a core self is necessary *before* one can "*enter into or use* the transitional spaces" (emphasis mine) that are so much a part of the mobile and multiple subject. "Core" self here is clearly a self in process, and cohering in no way suggests a necessary closure, or an absolutely fixed identity, but rather a basis from which to interact with one's contexts. The "transition space" that Flax names can be "entered into" or "used" as that zone or site in which a "knowing self" is experienced as knower and (un)known, engendered and ambivalent, embodied and imagined.

Rather than figuring subjectivity as a "center" or "core" of a person, I read the texts of feminist autography as articulating not a site or a space, but an energy. It is this "I" that works for the social, material, and personal transformations that we know as feminism, seeking an alternative both to the supression of difference that totalization implies and to the dissociations suggested by a fragmented subjectivity. Sidonie Smith observes that "endless fragmentation and a reified multiplicity" make the feminist subject an elusive being ("Autobiographical Manifesto" 188). She notes, "It is hard to coalesce a call to political action around a constantly deferred point of departure"

(188). Feminist gestures toward cohesion may be grounded in the desire for a "point of departure" and, indeed, a point of arrival, that embrace a process of transformation as a revolutionary concept, and as a feminist principle.

I situated "transformation" as epigraph to this chapter, and this book, in order to suggest how deeply embedded the idea and value of transformation are in the practice of feminist autography. If we agree that "no socio-political transformation is possible which does not constitute a transformation of subjects" (Kristeva quoted by Stanton, "Language" 74), we will agree with Catherine Belsey's observation about the intimate link between the social and the personal: "In the fact that the subject is a *process* lies the possibility of transformation" ("Constructing" 50). The subject as and in process is central to what I have been discussing here. In Gayatri Spivak's definition of feminism, bodies are involved in action, whereas transformation seems to be primarily a mental phenomenon (*"against* sexism, where women unite as a biologically oppressed caste; and *for* feminism, where human beings train to prepare for a transformation of consciousness" (*In Other Worlds* 144). Gloria Anzaldúa corrects the balance and returns us to women's bodies and the role of the body in transformations of consciousness and action: "For silence to transform into speech, sounds and words, it must first traverse through our female bodies" (*Making Face* xxii).

Transformation enters the discussion of writing the self in that it is the site of the mutable self engaging with language. When this multiple transformation includes the intention to effect social/cultural/political change, as an aspect of writing the self, feminist autography is quickened.

Rewriting the Real Body: Audre Lorde

It is against this background of transformation that I wish to set my discussion of Audre Lorde's *The Cancer Journals*. Her writing of self is both the account of a transformation of her body through cancer surgery and the reconstruction, textually, of her sense of self. Alicia Ostriker, basing her assertion on a study of hundreds of American

poets, observes that "when a woman poet today says 'I,' she is likely
to mean herself, as intensely as her imagination and her verbal skills
permit" (*Stealing the Language* 12). Although Ostriker does not prob-
lematize this "self," her distinction between the woman's voice saying
"I" and the depersonalized masks of the "I" as conventionally distanced figure speaks directly to the construction and articulation of
Lorde's feminist subjectivity. Sidonie Smith's important description
of "autobiographical manifestos" delimits "texts by women which participate in self-consciously political autobiographical acts" ("Autobiographical Manifesto" 189). Like autobiographical acts, autographical ones may be self-consciously political, and the "I" in both kinds
of works is in service to a new "social reality" (189).

In contrast to the rigorously shaped chronology and narrative co-
herence of *Zami* (even when autobiography is disturbed by "bio-
mythographic" elements), the dynamics of process evident in *The
Cancer Journals* suggests some aspects of the distinction I wish to
draw between autobiography and autography. This reading of *The
Cancer Journals* examines who and how Audre Lorde means when
she says "I."

In 1978, Audre Lorde had her right breast removed, having discovered it contained a malignant tumor. That cancer metastasized and
caused her death in November 1992. *The Cancer Journals,* published
in 1980, is her writing of the experience of breast cancer and her understanding of it in its social context. It is a slim volume composed
of personal exposition, a speech, essays, and a selection of dated journal entries, embedded in and set off from the main text in italics.
The writing of this text exemplifies Ostriker's view that "when defining a personal identity women tend to begin with their bodies" (11).
The site of self-as-object, to be seen, as well as subject, experiencing
and experienced, the body becomes the locus of tension about identity: "I have a body" struggles with "I am a body." Lorde's surgery left
her with the realization that, in her words, "I am who the world and
I have never seen before" (48). In this assertion, Lorde is allied with
"the world" as specularizer gazing at the unfamiliar external self, and
is simultaneously reconstructing a self who is a recipient of the gaze.
The doubly mirroring "I" is ontologically changed as her body is

changed, and the "I am who" requires an internal and external revision of knowledge. In contrast both to the Platonic and Christian ideals of a transcendent disembodied state[23] and to the panic of the postmodern condition in which "the body ... has *already* disappeared, and what we experience as the body is only a fantastic simulacra of body rhetorics" (Kroker and Kroker, *Body Invaders* 21–22), Lorde's real breast has been disappeared, and not as rhetoric. Her will to *"think through the body,* to connect what has been so cruelly disorganized" (Rich, *Of Woman Born* 284) removes "the" body from a category of abstraction and brings the idea of body alongside the fact of it.

For Lorde, the "fact" of her body is imbricated with the weight of a racist context in which, as bell hooks points out, "black women ... internalize the assumption that we/our bodies do not need care" (*Sisters* 88). The conflation of "we" and "our bodies" that hooks makes on behalf of African American women is intensified in her assertion that "care of the self begins with our capacity to tenderly and lovingly care for the body" (88).[24] Lorde's will to care for her self refuses the "fantastic simulacra" that encode denial of body as self.

In the period of decision before surgery Lorde describes the "concert of voices" inside herself. She understands the discordant "voices" as "those myriad pieces of myself and my background and experience and definitions of myself I had fought so long and hard to nourish and maintain" (31). These "pieces of self" do not have to function as a unified, coherent whole, perhaps because of the presence of the "I" who fights for their right to be heard. The multitude is full of contradictions: one "thin high voice was screaming that none of this was true" (30); another detached itself and provided a cool commentary; yet another demanded sleep. Lorde does not distinguish how she identifies an "I" who listens to the many voices of her selves, but certain entries from the journal of the time reveal that no central "I," separate from the other parts of self, maintained a consistent presence, a transcendent control. The deep subjectivity functions as an "ear" to the voices, and as an arbiter, counting costs. Of her decision to have a mastectomy, for example, Lorde says, "I would have paid more than even my beloved breast ... to preserve that self that was not merely physically defined" (32). Yet the surgery, as the journal entry at the time shows, is modifying that undefined but "real" self: *"I want to write of the pain I am feeling right now, of the lukewarm tears that will not stop coming into my eyes—for what? For my lost breast? For the lost me? And which me was that again anyway?... I want to be the person I used to be, the real me"* (October 10, 1978, 24–25). Physical pain, and the desire to make that immediate in the writing, is diverted into the psychic pain of loss. Longing for the familiar and the known, speaking from the position of the estranged, and consequently (in this moment) the less "real," Lorde struggles to accept all the "me's" — even the ones that contradict her belief that one self is as "real" as another.

Lorde encourages a multiplicity of selves, and the spirals of selves (Black, lesbian, feminist, mother, poet) that touch, meet, cross, and blur according to context must all be given voice. These "selves" could be considered "discourses"; that is, they could be the complex of what one says about one's Blackness, for example — how it means, how it is interpreted/understood/experienced. But, when seen as "discourse," the self loses its link to the body, to the self indicated but not (or not yet) written. To think of self as merely discourse seems arid, and to choose "discourse" as the dominant trope for discussing *this* I, this writing, is to disfigure the passion with which Lorde allies her written self to her physical self.[25]

The day after the stitches were removed, she wrote:

> *The act of writing seems impossible to me sometimes, the space of time for the words to form or be written is long enough for the situation to totally alter, leaving you liar or at search once again for the truth. What seems impossible is made real/tangible by the physical form of my brown arm moving across the page; not that my arm cannot do it, but that something holds it away.* (October 5, 1978, 52)

Here the physical act of writing parallels the emotional/psychological impossibility of expression. The immobility of Lorde's "brown arm" represents for her the slipperiness of her understanding and the objectification of the seen, dissociated from the seer. The dislocation and fragmentation of self into parts, first person into second ("I" into "you"), and word from feeling ("leaving you liar"), all must be recorded, but the fragmentation is left unreified. As an aspect of her responsibility to her "own selves," Lorde resists conclusion, waiting to understand, she says, "how I feel to my selves" (65). No particular voice seems to come forward with a truth that holds steadily for this time, and the traumatized selves resist language: "*There is so much I have not said in the past few days, that can only be lived now —*" (October 5, 1978, 52). What is too elusive or inchoate to be spoken in the moment (in the journal) is returned to and given account of in the writing that lies alongside the italicized entries. Lorde explains, "I am writing this now in a new year, recalling, trying to piece together that chunk of my recent past, so that I, or anyone else in need or desire, can dip into it at will if necessary to find the ingredients with which to build a wider construct. That is an important function of the telling of experience" (53). Positioning herself as witness, Lorde enacts the testimonial as "a discursive *practice,* as opposed to a pure *theory*" (Felman and Laub, *Testimony* 5). The self-reflexivity of Lorde's text brings her desire for transparency, for a useful telling of the past, into tense collusion with her refusal to allow her history to be a self-contained whole. Lorde's text brings its own "transparent intelligibility" (*Testimony* 174) into question as it circles her explanations, approaching her experience from different perspectives at different times. She is both reader and writer of her text, witness to the writing as well as to the layers of lived experience. Witnessing, then, becomes an act and an art "partaking of the very physicality of Resistance" (Felman and Laub 109, n. 9), as the writing becomes a necessary part of living her self. In part this is an aspect of her political life — both her act of resistance and her making of a community through transforming what is usually seen as private experience into a public matter. Yet, her own individual concerns are of equal importance to her: "I am also writing to sort out for myself who I was and was becoming throughout that time" (53). The previous selves (here in the journal entries as well as in the memories) come into play with the present writing self. Lorde's insistent drawing of attention to the fact of writing/the act of writing — whether in the past or at the moment — layers this text, and allows Lorde terrific flexibility. Within a page, Lorde includes details of memory ("I would sleep for a few hours and then I would get up, go to the john, write down my dreams on little scraps of paper without my glasses" [52]; rational thoughts ("I'd remember that we have always been temporary" [52]; a journal entry, always dated and italicized, clearly an interpolated text (*"I feel like I'm counting my days in milliseconds"* [October 5, 1978, 52]); and an abrupt move into the present ("I am writing this across a gap so filled with death — real death, the fact of it — that it is hard to believe that I am still . . . alive and writing this" [53]). The tensions/links among the italicized journal entries, the memories, and the controlled exposition of the "main" text conveys the various tensions and links that Lorde herself experiences: the threatened, physically damaged and traumatized self, and the later, ongoing self, the survivor who has selected the journal entries and other interpolations, and decided which selves will make up the present text. Transitions between the period of physical and emotional crisis and the occasion it gives Lorde for examining yet another perspective on the ways all women's lives and bodies are shaped carry the weight of self-in-process. Lorde's will to make her life, her body, and her text have meaning through the force of her own shaping power refutes the notion that "will" acts monodimensionally. Listening and speaking are aspects of voice and of writing self.

Lorde addresses this complexity explicitly, giving the matter a significance it rarely carries. In the introduction, reflecting on the discovery of a malignant tumor in her breast, she describes the fear that now attends a cough or a bruise as "another malignancy" (15). Her reaction is to transform this fear into language, for "the fears are most powerful when they are not given voice" (15). But it is this transformation into language, this giving voice, that catches Lorde in a terrifying double bind:

> I write so much here about fear because in shaping this introduction to *The Cancer Journals,* I found fear laid across my hands like a steel bar. When I tried to reexamine the 18 months since my mastectomy, some of what I touched was molten despair and waves of mourning — for my lost breast, for time, for the luxury of false power. Not only were these emotions difficult and painful to relive, but they were entwined with the terror that if I opened myself once again to scrutiny, to feeling the pain of loss, of despair, . . . then I might also open myself again to disease. (15–16)

The link between writing the self, here the self afflicted with cancer, and *being* that self is so powerful that Lorde fears that recreating the time in words may recreate it in her body. This fear speaks out of an integrated sense of mind, emotion, and body. The self that experienced the disease, the self that survived it, and the self that writes it may coalesce, beginning the cycle again. Time does not collapse — but the conditions, mental and emotional, are similar, and for Lorde, fear accompanies her awareness that the writing re-presents and may re-create the constellation of her life at the onset of cancer. Necessary for her integrity, however, is her ability to transform feeling into action, fear into language. This drive requires her to remember that she "had known the pain, and survived it," and "it only remained . . . to give it voice, to share it for use, that the pain not be wasted" (16). The writing of self, then, is useful for knowing herself for herself, but the transformation of her experience into writing is to make the experience useful to other women as well. A privately held experience is one held in silence, and an imposed silence is an enemy of community.

Following the introduction (written in late August 1980), in which she gives a kind of summary of the previous two years, Lorde opens the body of the book with a piece of writing called "The Transformation of Silence into Language and Action." It originally was a speech Lorde gave in 1977[26] after her first cancer biopsy showed a breast tumor to be benign, not malignant. Pathos suffuses these words, written in relief and strength, since the introduction already has told us that a year later a malignant tumor would be discovered. But their inclusion is not for sentimental or ironic excitements; rather it shows the use she makes of her experience for her political (that is, Black lesbian feminist) values. She reviews her past fears or hesitations: "To question or to speak as I believed could have meant pain, or death. . . . Death . . . is the final silence. And that might be coming quickly, now, without regard for whether I had ever spoken . . . or had only betrayed myself into small silences" (20). Lorde's realization is phrased in intensely personal language: "I was going to die, if not sooner then later, whether or not I had ever spoken myself" (20). Silence betrays the self, and speaking the self is an action, one resisting the "final silence" of death and the everyday silences of self-betrayal. If death is silence then life must be (in part at least) language, and giving the self in language, or to language, is a death-defying act.

But the physical death that comes to all is not the most important one in Lorde's view. The "tyrannies of silence" imposed by social and political structures determine whose voices should be heard, and whose words can have an effect. To speak the self (in Lorde's iconography) is to make oneself a warrior. The women who sustained her as she waited for the biopsy results were, she says, "black and white, old and young, lesbian, bisexual, and heterosexual, and we all shared a war against the tyrannies of silence" (20). We must recall that Lorde here is making a presentation as a Black lesbian, an unapologetic radical feminist, in a conventional though liberal, mostly white context (an MLA conference), and she speaks of her fears: "And of course I am afraid—you can hear it in my voice—because the transformation of silence into language and action is an act of self-revelation that always seems fraught with danger" (21). It may be obvious that the imagery of war, tyranny, and warriors comes from fear (as well as courage), but Lorde marks the danger of self-revelation as a given ("of course I am afraid"). The danger is clear: speaking/putting ourselves into words exposes us, makes us visible, and that opens us to various threats, some of them material. Cautioning against too great a trust in the political efficacy of the seen, Peggy Phelan argues that visibility "summons surveillance and the law; it provokes voyeurism, fetishism, the colonialist/imperial appetite for possession" (*Unmarked,* 1993 6). But Lorde's concerns exceed her misgivings about losing the advantages of invisibility. Apart from the external dangers, Lorde says, "I think we fear the very visibility without which we cannot truly live" (21). To be heard is to be seen in Lorde's argument, and the claiming of speech exerts a measure of control (to "truly live" must mean some power over representations of self) that the grammar of "being seen" disallows.

Lorde makes the general "we" of women into the more particular "we" of connection with Black women: "black women have on the one hand always been highly visible," and on the other "been rendered invisible through the depersonalization of racism" (21). The alternative to breaking silence is to remain "mute forever while our sisters and ourselves are wasted, while our children are distorted and destroyed, while our earth is poisoned" (22). The "we" shifts back into an inclusive embrace, and she invites the whole audience into that embrace: "We must each of us recognize our responsibility to seek those words [of women] out ... not hide behind the mockeries of separation that have been imposed upon us" (23). Lorde concludes, "It is not difference which immobilizes us, but silence" (23). Difference lives in the realm of the visible, silence in the realm of language. From her personal or private invisibility/fear/silence Lorde opens outward to the experience of other women, not only those who are like her in specific ways (Black, lesbian, facing death from breast cancer), but to any who are conscious of the fear imposed by the tyranny of silences. In this oratorical exhortation, Lorde makes the revelation of her own, embodied self the ground of her urging. Being seen (the visibility necessary for life) is emancipatory only in the context of her own words. Her own fear becomes exemplary, and her words become the actions she calls for in her rage for transformations.

The second section of *The Cancer Journals* is titled "Breast Cancer: A Black Lesbian Feminist Experience" (24–54). Jerome Brooks dismisses the "Black, Lesbian, Feminist" aspects as irrelevant to the general female experience of breast cancer,[27] but he is absurdly wrong. Not only are *The Cancer Journals* the particular experiences of a particular woman who happens to be Black, lesbian, and feminist. But the *ways* Lorde interprets her experience (that is, how she experiences) are shaped by the discourses of those identities. For Lorde the categories are the languages of her selves, and much of the writing is making that precise point explicit. Moreover, the material context in which she lives through the events that she is recounting is a female community with all the resources that a feminist context can provide. Lorde lists the names of women who in innumerable ways made themselves available for her, her lover, and her children during the crisis and afterward. What made breast cancer the occasion for a more intense selfhood was the fact of feminist[28] systems of support. Lorde's insisting on the list of differences is an aspect of affirming them (and that Brooks reads it as a kind of aggression to see the chapter named thus indicates the weight and ubiquity of silencings—which is how I read that Black male scholar's refusal to take seriously Lorde's specifying of her identities). Consistently in these writings Lorde connects silence with suppressed differences and language with transformation.

Lorde provides precisely detailed information that is often withheld about the physical and emotional effects of the mutilating surgery she underwent. Words, however, are not Lorde's only means of action. She speaks of her body, but she also allows it to speak its own difference. Breast cancer and the (common) result of it, breast removal, are veiled and silenced. Women who have had a breast removed are expected, even required, to hide the fact, performing an image of the unhurt female body for public consumption. Lorde refuses a prosthesis, a false breast. Within a few days of her surgery (grim descriptions of the pain and misery preceded this passage), Lorde is visited by a friendly lady from Reach for Recovery bearing a pale pink ("flesh-colored") false breast:

> Her message was, you are just as good as you were before because you can look exactly the same ... nobody will ever know the difference. But what she said was, "You'll never know the difference," and she lost me right there, because I knew sure as hell I'd know the difference. (42)

Lorde is wry on the subject of difference here: the Reach for Recovery woman opens her jacket and displays "her two considerable breasts" in a tight blue sweater, challenging Lorde, "Now can you tell which is which?" Lorde says, "I admitted that I could not. In her tight foundation garment and stiff up-lifting bra, both breasts looked equally unreal to me" (42). Rejecting the unreality of a false breast is rejecting a lie, in Lorde's terms; it is erasing the difference between herself and women who have not undergone a mastectomy. She stuffs the pink pad into the right side of the bra she had been given: "It perched on my chest askew, awkwardly inert and lifeless, and having nothing to do with any me I could possibly conceive of" (44). It is not the absurdity of the bit of padded lambswool and nylon, pink against her brown skin that repels Lorde. She says that not even "the most skillfully designed prosthesis in the world" could undo the reality of amputation, or feel the way her breast had felt. Her own requirements are clear to her: "Either I would love my body one-breasted now, or remain forever alien to myself" (44).

She does learn to love herself, again, but her account of the hostility and disgust she meets from doctors, nurses, other women (she does not speak of general male response) shows how difficult the celebration of difference is, and loudly her body speaks it. She describes the day, some time after the surgery, when she goes to the doctor (a specialist in breast cancers) for a checkup, without a prosthesis. She walks in "with that brave new-born security of a beautiful woman having come through a very hard time and being very glad to be alive" wearing one dramatic earring "in the name of grand asymmetry" (58). The dismayed nurse explains that to show the absence of a breast is bad for patients' "morale" (60). To reject the prosthesis is not only to reject the foreign object. It is to reject the right of society to decide how a woman must be as a body. She refuses, as a feminist, the view that how her body looks is the most important part of a woman, and that the external objectific(a)tion must be adhered to by every woman. Lorde mourns the loss of her right breast, not as appearance, or as an aspect of her image, but the "feeling and the fact" (65) of it. Her analysis and rejection of the "wipe-out of self" (64) that an externalized sense of self demands of women, and the part that "Cancer Inc." (62) plays in that "wipe-out" are framed in the language of female autonomy. She affirms her own subjecthood, and deciding to live in her body without disguise is part of her integrating the private and public aspects of female selfhood. The promise that "nobody will know the difference" is precisely Lorde's objection to the prosthesis. She wants to affirm, not veil, differences; and by showing herself as different, that is, as one-breasted, she makes herself visible to other women. Her body speaks to them of difference, the same difference that many women live in silence.

The Cancer Journals is Lorde's way to assert her right "to define and claim" (59) her own body, and to complete the process of the new self that the first cancer biopsy initiated. Notions of wholeness and unity of self are simultaneously affirmed and disrupted here as the brutal (and graphically described [36]) surgery leaves Lorde with the belief that "in the process of losing a breast I had become a more whole person" (55). The irregular movement of this matrix of becoming more and less whole, and the voices Lorde brings to its inscription, makes *The Cancer Journals* textually complicated. The introduction starts with Lorde's conclusions, her physical survival, and her intentions to prevent another "imposed silence" from acting on women as a "tool for separation and powerlessness" (9). Her personal needs and her political aims coalesce here and the text makes her rhetorical assertions and her personal journal entries link different aspects of her experience. The body of the text, following the introduction, concentrates on various issues, but all sections parallel the opening movements with a mixture of essay-narrative, recountings, journal entries, and informal conversational passages. The chronology is mixed. The final chapter, the most politically analytic of the role that the "Cancer Establishment" (58) plays in the lives of women, begins at the beginning: "On Labor Day, 1978, during my monthly self-examination, I discovered a lump in my right breast" (55). And the language itself takes many forms: some have the flavor of kitchen-table intimacies, as in the description of her postsurgery feelings ("*I found I could finally masturbate again, making love to myself for hours*" (November 2, 1978, 25). Other journal passages are formal, ritualized, carrying the echo of the preacher: "*What is there possibly left for us to be afraid of, after we have dealt face to face with death and not embraced it?*" (December 29, 1978, 25). Some sections are in plain expository prose, informative with few flourishes of lyricism or exhortation, certainly reflecting a practical mind at work: "I considered the alternatives of the straight medical profession, surgery, radiation, chemotherapy. I considered the holistic approaches of diet, vitamin therapy" (30).

This text spirals — Lorde writes layer after layer of the experience, no single issue allowed to dominate the others: death, cancer, surgery, and the attendant fear and pain; repetitions of hope, feminist support, and understanding; the cycles of relationship of selves in her body and in the world and as a representative of other women and their experience; and, consistently, her refusal to "waste" the experience, that is, her self, in privacy, in silence. The self (or selves) of

Audre Lorde in her various manifestations appearing here makes for a writing that lives close to the vulnerable and uncertain flesh, and yet enjoys rhetorical authority, sureness, and even righteousness. *The Cancer Journals* is the transformation of all that into a powerful text of feminist subjectivity.

The Cancer Journals is a crucial text for understanding what I mean by "autography" because of the ways in which the text makes up the self it articulates. Unconstrained by generic expectations, that text produces a subjectivity that asserts as well as interrogates the ground of its own being. The selfhood that Lorde moves toward is both represented in and constituted by her volume. But while Lorde's *Journals* is exemplary, it is not representative of feminist autography. No piece of writing could be. Each text makes its own processes, establishing its own ground and taking up its own subjectivity as the self and the writing enter and reconfigure feminist communities.

CHAPTER TWO

Adrienne Rich:
A Poetics of Subjectivity

Adrienne Rich marks her later self-writing with an insistence on the specificity of place and the unforgivingness of time. The intersections of time and place that Rich makes are more than gestures toward history. In Rich's poetry, as in her prose, her desire to "change the laws of history" ("Sources" 23) presses her into a dialectic of ethical self-positioning. The "laws of history," that is, the laws that serve few at the cost of many, the laws that make wars inevitable, the laws of the Fathers, are inscribed on and within each person, and are the expected trajectories of lives and native lands. Conventional paradigms of history—as a reified narrative of significant events, as a fiction of progress, or as an ongoing class or caste struggle—do not dominate Rich's thinking about history, although they may offer structures from which alterity could be developed. The fierce attention that her writing gives to the past does not stand above experience, gesturing toward moments as monuments, but rather asserts an embeddedness of meaning within time, both the past and the present. To change the laws of history, Rich suggests, the past must be known, that is, made emotionally intelligible. Shoshana Felman,

reading Camus, notes that "the artist's role is to demolish the decep-
tive image of history as an *abstraction* ... by *bearing witness to the
body*" (Felman and Laub, *Testimony* 108). The body of the witness as
well as that of the bearer of history's effects works against abstraction. Responsibility for the shaping power of vision ensures that the
perspective of the "seer" is made an aspect of what is seen. The
process of knowing is in part "counting the cost" (Rich, "Contradictions" 100), being accountable for and to the circles that overlap between past and present, the individual and the familial, the cultural
and the political.

My reading of Rich will examine the strategies by which her recurring passions (history, the body) become the written self that
claims multiplicity without evacuating presence. Both the poems and
the prose speak aspects of self into being and then into dialogue. She
begins the poem "Integrity" with the *Webster's* definition of that word
(*"the quality or state of being complete; unbroken condition; entirety"*)
then re-creates what "being complete" might mean. She recognizes
physical landmarks, then dismisses their importance, as this journey
brings her to a realization: "but really I have nothing but myself / to
go by" and then reflects in another, italicized voice, *"Nothing but
myself?... My Selves. /* After so long, this answer" (*Fact* 273–74). In
this poem, the selves are experienced as "anger and tenderness: my
selves," which, she says, "breathe in me / as angels not polarities."

Rich comes repeatedly to the assertion of a multiple and complex
subjectivity. The "self" *is* "selves," though not always figured as angels, and Rich's commitment to a textualized presence-of-self-to-self
shapes the ontological problematic of her poetry and her prose.

The aspect of Rich's autography that I will consider here examines her analytic re-visions and poetic constructions of her own past
and the conceptions of self-in-history that she produces. In the first
section I discuss various prose essays that demonstrate her shifting
perceptions of the "selves" placed in time. These self-reflexive essays
are structured by the ethical imperative to act as witness to injus-
tices, both external and internalized. Then I consider the later long
poems "Sources" and "Contradictions: Tracking Poems" and use other

works to suggest some ways that the cartographies of poetic speech map an "I" informed by all its geopolitical, sexual, embodied attentions, and shaped by relationships. Her changing "worldview has required certain shifts in her poetics," which Rich has worked out, Thomas Byers notes, "by rewriting herself" (152). In both the prose and the poetry, Rich's historicized feminist sensibility rewrites her self and thus makes a poetics of subjectivity.

Rich repeatedly has tried to answer her own question, "What kind of beast would turn its life into words?" ("21 Love Poems," *Fact* 239). For Rich, the composition of a "self" occurs in the act of writing. But that composition is not just the assemblage of parts that lie fragmented. Self-representation rather gives words to external and internal silence, resisting the forces that have made so much of "woman's story a story of silence, powerlessness, self-effacement" (Smith, *Poetics* 53). Telling women's stories, including her own, means both naming the violations and oppressions *and* retelling the stories that escaped the grasp of silence, those that had a voice, but no public listener.

These tracings do not contain the person any more than any map contains a country, but — perhaps — no less. In "Delta" (1987) Rich reminds me of what every reader of subjectivity must never forget: the "I" is there in the poem and is not; "Rich" is the poet/speaker, but that speaking is not Rich:

> If you have taken this rubble for my past
> raking through it for fragments you could sell
> know that I long ago moved on
> deeper into the heart of the matter
> If you think you can grasp me, think again:
>
> my story flows in more than one direction
> a delta springing from the riverbed
> with its five fingers spread (TP 32)

What interests me here about this poem is the varied "selvings" (Du-Plessis 99) at work in it. The reader who positions herself as archaeologist is challenged, mocked, for seeing the poem as mere trashy sediment. Nevertheless, it is Rich's voice that declares the poems a waste, broken bits of old structures. The "rubble" of these poems once held her — contained or interested her? — but no longer: "I long ago moved on." Refusing fossilization, resisting commodification, this "I" is, however, here, and seems to have returned to speak long-distance from an imagined future that could not have been known at the moment of writing but that since has been inhabited by that same speaking "I." The direction of the movement downward, "deeper into the heart of the matter," lies alongside the image of the delta, "springing" up from the riverbed (another heart?). Here "me," "my past," and "my story" come together and flow apart. As the "I" channels deeper, the "me," self as object, eludes grasp, spreading widely. The tension, almost anger, in these few lines addressed to a reader whose aim is to "grasp," whose intention is to "sell," provides a cautionary edge to Rich's self-scape.

For Rich, feminist consciousness, independence from poetic conventions, and articulation of a personal self coalesce in the shift she made from the formal poetic structures, in which she did not yet dare to say "I" in a poem ("When We Dead," *On Lies* 45), to a writing in which using "I" marks the affirmation and consequent transformation of self as part of, yet distinct from, her context. Reiteration and repetition, necessary to resist the weight of silence and the effect of erasure, is part of writing "I." Another equally important aspect of Rich's autography is her marking of self-difference, over time, as "Delta" suggests, and within a given moment. The assertion or insertion of self, and of the right to speak the self, must be repeated as self changes. How that happens is what I will explore.

The Prose

LOCUS OF POWER, LOCUS OF SHAME

Like Audre Lorde, Rich experiences danger in speaking the self "when those who have the power to name and to socially construct reality choose not to see you or hear you" ("Invisibility," *Blood* 199). Discovering at a public lecture that once more her lesbianism is an unspoken, invisible part of her — despite the fact that she has been "for ten years a very visible lesbian" — she says:

> This experience has reminded me of what I should never have let myself
> forget: that invisibility is not just a matter of being told to keep your
> private life private, it's the attempt to fragment you, to prevent you from
> integrating, love and work and feeling and ideas, with the empowerment
> that that can bring. ("Invisibility," *Blood* 200)

With the collapse of "I" and "you" Rich affirms the impersonality of
oppression. Whoever the individual is, she must resist invisibility, silence. The link, in Lorde and now here, between being seen and being heard suggests a breakdown of the distance/dichotomy between
the body in its three dimensions and the voice or language (or writing). Here the displacement of the person by print is not at all an issue. Here the self in writing, in language, in public is in no way a
negation or denigration (or a defacement) of self. Rather it is the
place of transformation made accessible to others: to speak the fragmentation, the suppression, is to resist it, to refuse it, and thus to
make a gesture of integration—this is one aim of transformation.
To write, for example, "I am a lesbian" is to take the power of naming that self. In contrast to the notion that "the conceit of autonomy
implied by self-naming is the paradigmatically presentist conceit ...
the belief that there is a one who arrives in the world, in discourse,
without a history" (Butler, *Bodies* 228), Rich's self-namings invariably take her to history and to connection. As the "I" and the "you"
are mutually bound here in the need to link *our* "love and work and
feelings and ideas" ("Invisibility," *Blood* 200), Rich's refusal to be
silent about the resonance of shared self-naming embraces readers
who (feel they) have not the power to name themselves.

Like silence, the issue of fragmentation is integral to her mature
poetry. She speaks of the process of integration in her poetry of
the late 1960s: "I began to resist the apparent splitting of poet from
woman, thinker from woman, and to write what I feared was political poetry" ("Blood," *Blood* 176). The multiple selves that she
speaks of elsewhere are not so easily divisible either into roles (mother,
poet, etc.) or into socially divisible functions.[1] The resistance here
is grounded in a refusal of public definitions of a "woman" and in
a longing for a personal, embodied, engendered vision. In early
"political poetry" (antiwar, pro–civil rights), Rich found "little loca-

tion of the self, the poet's own identity as man or woman," and "felt driven — for [her] own sanity — to bring together in [her] poems" politics ("out there") and "supposedly private" life ("Blood," *Blood* 181).

The long evolution of Rich's consciousness of the relations of poetry to political and personal presence is an exciting study of "the dynamic between poetry as language and poetry as a kind of action" (181). Rich's evolution is not, however, my immediate concern. Rather, I wish to consider her later essays and poetry in order to track the various provisional selves (the contradictions and continuities of the self) as Rich herself does. Rich's writing of a feminist self as a political, sociocultural phenomenon describes past selves with confidence in some pieces and uncertainty in others. The present speaking self is at times sure and analytic, at others troubled and grappling. Whatever the tone or mood of Rich's writing, no aspect of the self is exempt from considerations of class, race, gender, sexual identity — the relations of power and her place(s) in the power structures, and in history.

In her prose, Rich seems stuck in historical responsibilities. To know and to name herself is to place herself in categories — Jewish, lesbian, white, American[2] — and then to examine her differences from and differences within the distinctive groups, whether they be marginal or dominant. For Rich these groupings are ways of knowing herself and ways of being in the world, and her essays explore the epistemologies of selfhood allowed and required, or suppressed, by taking on the self as part of a larger context. She examines the sexual and racial dynamics of the United States, and the ways those forces divide women against each other and within themselves. Rich's autobiographical material (often used as illustration or example) in some of her early feminist writing[3] is conventional in that she seems to treat the present summations as the "true" story. Yet Rich consistently asserts that any moment of fixity is provisional; always the possibility of change, of revision is affirmed/inherent in the prose. The belief that any single telling of a story is sufficient is inimical to Rich's belief that "truthfulness anywhere means a heightened complexity. But it is a movement into evolution. Women are only beginning to uncover our own truths; many of us would be grateful for some rest in that struggle" ("Women," *On Lies* 193). In "evolution," exposure and change are inextricable. For Rich the "hearing and saying of women" breaks silence within our selves, and transforms "forever the way we see" ("Motherhood," *On Lies* 260). This is an ongoing process, never complete. Experiencing the sharp pleasure of "uncovering" something true for oneself, in contrast to the oppression of living under the covers of someone else's truth, is addictive, though exhausting. The desire for rest in that struggle, which Rich articulated in 1975, and the relentlessness of uncovery, testify to Rich's prescience. Speaking those discoveries becomes a transformation, in stages, of self as a feminist imperative. Within the context of community and history, then, the feminist self changes and is changed as breaking silence, putting self into words, transforms reality.

The membrane between the self as part of a group and the self as a privately experienced, separate being is troublingly permeable. Increasingly, Rich affirms a politics of identity[4] in which the personal and the political displace each other repeatedly in any movement of identity or relationship. Rich brings this tension into play when she argues against abstraction of female experience. She speaks of "the body": "When I write 'the body,' I see nothing in particular. To write 'my body' plunges me into lived experience, particularity" ("Notes," *Blood* 215). She goes on to speak those particularities of that lived body, including the sociopolitical effects: "The teeth of a middle-class person seen by the dentist twice a year from childhood. White skin, marked and scarred by three pregnancies, an elected sterilization, progressive arthritis ... four joint operations" (215). This body is defined by what it has not lived, but was vulnerable to, as well: "no rapes, no abortions" (215). The self lived in this designated body is peculiarly impersonal. Again Barthes's "autobiography" is provocative: "You are the only one who can never see yourself except as an image .... especially for your own body, you are condemned to the repertoire of its images" (*Roland Barthes* 36). Generalized by class, and by the metaphor of race ("white" people do not really have white skin), the body of Adrienne Rich is here a phenomenon of external influences and events, and as a "self" is not an experienced being in this description. Rich says "I" and "my" of this body, yet her ways of speaking it are empirical, factual, rather than felt; however, this body is also not an image, not a looked-at object but a combination of reported events. Rich's aim in this essay (the title is significant: "Notes Toward a Politics of Location") is to take on her body as a political fact, the elemental location.[5] Her concern here is to combat the impulse to abstract, to universalize, that she finds in women writing "the body." The components of self (or the factors that constitute a social as well as personal identity) located in one's body are not in themselves singular, and all must be acknowledged and considered — not only as female fact and meaning: "It means recognizing this white skin, the places it has taken me, the places it has not let me go" (*Blood* 215–16).[6] For Rich, then, the "plunge" into lived experience that comes for her with saying "my body" is not necessarily experience to be written. Nevertheless, the particularities of her body place her in a context that she must, as part of her feminist ethics, take into account and be accountable to and for.

Her body is not the only factor in this process. To know/live/write her self, Rich has to explore[7] or discover or create her self as a Jew. She opens the essay "Split at the Root: An Essay on Jewish Identity" (*Blood* 100) with awareness of her fear. She places herself physically and emotionally, "sitting chin in hand in front of the typewriter, staring out at the snow" (100). She is trying to "figure out why writing this seems to be so dangerous an act, filled with fear and shame" (100). Like Audre Lorde, Rich finds her emotion at the moment of writing instructive. The interspace between the living and the writing, the self and the text, is charged with danger and fear. For Lorde, the source of fear is her reluctance to be visible, known. Rich, too, analyzes her fear: as an ardent and radical feminist, Rich wanted, like Virginia Woolf, to think back through [her] mothers, not her father.[8] To claim her Jewishness she must "claim" her father, and then break the silence he imposed on the fact of his Jewishness. The double movement of disloyalty she faces here — challenging a feminist rigidity by embracing her father as part of her self (though Rich was never a separatist, disburdening one's self of the father's mantle is necessarily part of a feminist development) and breaking his "taboos" by speaking as a

Jew — is insufficient to account for the fear and shame she feels at this writing. Rich must attend to "the third thing": "I have to face the sources and the flickering presence of my own ambivalence as a Jew; the daily mundane anti-Semitisms of my entire life" (100). To write this self (of her Jewish identity) is to make a mirror in which Rich faces a multiply mobile, consistent ("daily") but unstable ("flickering") self against self. Subjectivity is not merely taking up a "subject position" but is experiential, inhabiting a position in ways that dislocate images and habits of selfhood. The Other, here both male and Jew, must be claimed as a gesture toward wholeness, integrity, and away from silence, suppression. For Rich, autographics does not fix "self" and thus silence the interior Other, nor does her self-writing suppress conflicted feelings about either taking on or denying her Jewishness.

While the multiplicity of selves stands recognized, interrogated, from within and without, the written self is exposed as a kind of social metaphor. The silences within her about her own Jewishness lie parallel to the silent (and overt) anti-Semitism in her culture. Rich, then, comes to know herself as one might come to know another person. The difference is that the other whom Rich is coming to know is inextricably linked with the self she calls "I" in her lived experience and her written life. She writes as though she were talking to herself, as though her efforts to know herself are as important to us as to her, as though the reader is another self she is musing with:

> These are stories I never tried to tell before. Why, now? Why, I asked
> myself last year, does this question of Jewish identity float so impalpably,
> so ungraspably around me . . .
>   . . . And yet I've been on the track of this longer than I think. (100–101)

At the moment of writing, Rich has not "settled" the question of her Jewish identity, but she is in the midst of coming to know what she did not know she knew: the "stories" seem to be the lived experiences, not yet told, nor even attempted. Yet she has been on this "track" for longer than she knows, suggestively indicating the directions the unconscious self provides. "Track" (as in the later "tracking poems") signifies agency and desire, as in "to track" something elusive and needed, and then narrows to a noun, like a railway "track," inevitable, laid down, unyielding.

Repeatedly in Rich's writing the issue of choice appears, but having made a choice does not eliminate questions. In the midst of her examination of her ambivalences about Jewishness, she registers her impulse to silence the complexity both of her feelings and of the situation. She would like to take on an identity whole, and thus erase other, equally troubling parts of herself. Speaking of the "collusion" of white women with white men in the "southern racist scenario," for example, she says,

> It would be easy to push away and deny the gentile in me — that white southern woman, that social christian. At different times in my life I have wanted to push away one or the other burden of inheritance, to say merely *I am a woman; I am a lesbian.* (*Blood* 103)

Rich sometimes wishes to make her personal self and the political program of white feminism a perfect match, and to reduce to essentialist status the fact of being a woman, a lesbian, as though that were a simple identity. To do so, however, would be too close to the program Rich grew up with in the South. She describes the white, Christian world of family and social context, in which having "ideals" or "manners" included "not hurting someone's feelings by calling her or him a Negro or a Jew — naming the hated identity" (104). To name, then, is once more to make visible, apparent, things that already may be perfectly obvious but can remain in the realm of the unmarked unless they are labeled.

Following these disclosures about her family's cultural practices, she writes, "(Writing this I feel dimly like the betrayer: of my father ... of my mother ... of my caste and class; of my whiteness itself)" (104). We must remain conscious not only that this is *a* writing, that a single person sits writing (with whatever complex of discourses that are available to her at the time), but also that this writing produces effects that then also become part of the self, and therefore must also be written. That Rich's writing here is, indeed, autography rather than autobiography is indicated by the parenthetical passage. Rich maintains a distinction between what was then and what is now through the use of the parenthesis. The intrusion into her ongoing text does not disrupt it or dislocate it, but rather affirms both what she is saying about the lines drawn, the walls built between what can be spoken and what cannot, and that the individual carries and recreates those early impressions. Whiteness, then, is not merely a fact, but a stand, and to expose its secrets, the lessons on "ideals" or "manners" learned in an intellectual and liberal family, is to betray it. Rich's deep revulsion against racism cannot silence the racist voices of her internal context; in fact, they must be exposed; and in giving those voices a language, more aspects of her self are available for transformation.

AMNESIA AND THE ETHICS OF BETRAYAL

Guilt, and shame for feeling guilty, are not the only emotions this writing of her childhood arouses. She describes watching, at the age of sixteen, the documentary newsreels of the liberation of prisoners from Nazi concentration camps and says, "Writing this now, I feel belated rage that I was so impoverished by the family and social worlds I lived in, that I had to figure out by myself what this did indeed mean for me" (107). Rich's emotional responses in the present writing to the past reveal that, like the past selves, the present self is complex, even contradictory, and that the writing makes the variations within the self known, and perhaps knowable. It is in the act of writing that Rich experiences her internalized shame at "betraying" the social codes of anti-Semitism, white supremacy, and intellectual graciousness. The betrayals that carry the deepest charge for Rich are not those of parental or social expectation, but those of the self,

> committed so repeatedly, so mundanely, that they leave no memory trace behind, only a growing residue of misery, of dull sedimented self-hatred. Often these take the form not of words but of silence. Silence before the joke at which everyone is laughing: the anti-woman joke, the racist joke, the anti-Semitic joke. Silence and then amnesia. (109)

Writing/speaking the self may be experienced emotionally as the sediment of childhood training. But the deeper betrayal of the self comes not in speaking but in being silent, and in accreting "self hatred," which is inevitable when fear controls response. Teresa de Lauretis speaks of the "continuing significance, for feminism, of a 'politics of the unconscious'; for women's consent [to femininity] may not be gotten easily but it is finally gotten, and has been for a long time, as much by rape and economic coercion as by the more subtle and last-ing effects of ideology, representation, and identification" (*Alice Does-n't* 134). The "amnesia" that follows silence may be metaphorical here, but elsewhere Rich has written: "Amnesia is the silence of the un-conscious ... to lie habitually, as a way of life, is to lose contact with the the unconscious.... Lying is done with words, and also with si-lence" ("Women," *On Lies* 186–87). Connections within self, or of self with self, are damaged, disrupted with the lies/betrayals of si-lence. These disruptions create an internal silence that Rich calls am-nesia — very simply, one could be said to forget one's self.

Remembering the silenced/forgotten/denied/betrayed parts of one's self does not, however, bring the self into easy harmony. Rich is trou-bled by the impossibility of wholeness:

> Sometimes I feel I have seen too long from too many disconnected angles: white, Jewish, anti-Semite, racist, anti-racist, once-married, lesbian, middle-class, feminist, exmatriate southerner, *split at the root*— that I will never bring them whole. I would have liked, in this essay, to bring together the meanings of anti-Semitism and racism as I have experienced them and as I believe they intersect the world beyond my life. But I'm not able to do this yet. ("Split," *Blood* 122)

Her personal self, attitudes, values, experiences are gathered and listed here, not only as aspects of self, but as ethical and political issues. "In this essay" seems an important phrase: the writing about/of Jew-ish identity was to create a Jewish identity more comfortable than the one Rich had yet developed. But the effort could not succeed for her as individual, nor as political commentator. She writes:

> I am not able to do this yet. I feel the tension as I think, make notes: *If you really look at one reality, the other will waver and disperse....* Sometimes I feel inadequate to make any statement as a Jew; I feel the denial of history within me like an injury. (122)

Always the language is the place of possibility, of anxiety, of loss — and the place of wish. Again, taking the risk of entering language carries ethical significance. Rich makes a very delicate balance in the conclusion of this essay, confessing her inability to "bring them whole" while affirming her right/responsibility to speak: "We can't wait for the undamaged to make our connections for us; we can't wait to speak until we are perfectly clear" (123). Personal speaking shifts to communal speech: "I" becomes "we" as Rich invokes feminist practice, and surrenders herself to the generous critique of a community that understands that "we can't wait to speak." To take on the silenced and denied aspects of self is, for Rich, to enlarge the "range of accountability." "This essay," she says, "is another beginning for me" (123), one that demonstrates what she means when she speaks of accountability as engaging every aspect of (her) identity.

That engagement requires of Rich an examination of her life in language and denies even language as a safe place. Her range of accountability takes her from silence and denial into speech. But it requires her as a poet to acknowledge that the language she has been using is not necessarily trustworthy, or that an aesthetics of language may be an insufficient standard (beauty is not necessarily truth). She speaks of herself as "the poet who knows that beautiful language can lie, that the oppressor's language sometimes sounds beautiful" (123).

Rich moves from first-person singular to plural and finally to third person at the end of this essay as she lists her identities. This is a perplexing move in light of an earlier piece in which she speaks (again) of fear. Using herself as an an illustration of the process women writers go through, she describes the "deliberate detachment" with which she wrote, emphasizing the split between self as poet and self as woman, in some poems using "the persona of a man" ("When We Dead," *On Lies* 41). Even when she wrote from the position of a woman (an "extraordinary relief"), she says, "I hadn't found the courage yet ... to use the pronoun 'I' — the woman in the poem is always 'she'" (45). In more recent writing of both poems and prose Rich uses "I," but not invariably, and the gaps are suggestive. Roland Barthes sees a sinister aspect in speaking/writing about self in the third person: "To speak about oneself by saying 'he' can mean: *I am speaking about myself as though I were more or less dead* ... or again: I am speaking

about myself in the manner of the Brechtian actor who must distance his character: 'show' rather than incarnate him" (*Roland Barthes*
168). Barthes continues, "It annuls and mortifies its referent" (169).

Rich might agree that her early uses of the third person serve a
kind of possum effect. The self speaking plays dead and directs attention to a position or makes certain moves using "she" or even
"he" as a stand-in. But when the speaker is a feminist committed to
integration, and the third person is "she," does the same distancing,
the same annulment occur? In the concluding paragraph of "Split at
the Root" Rich says,

> I know that . . . every aspect of my identity will have to be engaged. The
> middle-class white girl. . . . The Jewish lesbian raised to be a heterosexual
> gentile. . . . The woman with three sons, the feminist who hates male
> violence. . . . The woman limping . . . The poet who knows. . . . The woman
> trying, as part of her resistance, to clean up her act. (*Blood* 123)

The "I" here in its various aspects becomes a medley of characters,
seen and described as from the outside. The difference between this
list of splittings and the earlier separations ("woman from poet,
woman from thinker") is that no one requires denial of the others:
the white girl, the woman, the poet, the Jewish lesbian, the feminist
are aspects of the one who says "my identity." The forces that Rich
uses are a repertoire of images, each held up in a kind of immobility.
Indeed, the splits and fragments of which Rich speaks seem here to
be frozen into the language of self-description, as characters independent of each other, uninforming and unforming of each other. The
"self" in this listing is displayed as a series of figures, as many third
persons, not incarnated with the fluidity of motion. This list could
have the effect of "eliminating the referent," Rich herself. Rich has
forestalled this response, however, with her earlier assertion of "we."
When she says "we can't wait to speak," she includes the women she
is, as well as the women she is not. It may be that the tension in Rich
between the various "shes" is that her relationship with (within) herself is akin to her relationship with other women. Barthes's "I" may
become a "he" or even a "you," but "we" is not in his repertoire of alternatives. When Barthes says of the use of the third person, "I always

envision a kind of murder by language ... whose entire scene ... is *gossip*" (169), he does not mean gossip as "emotional speculation" (Spacks, *Gossip* 3), but as dissection: the dismembering of the absent, hence vulnerable, other. He concentrates on the connotation of judgment by two persons of a third. When Rich displays the "aspects of her identity" in the third person, she is certainly presenting (and representing) herself for judgment, as accountable. The difference is that Rich is present in all her persons, singular and plural, first, second, and third. She speaks to the reader of "the woman who...," inviting assessment, while the parade of identities or "aspects" seems to diffuse focus. No one figure in the list can be singled out, yet each must be acknowledged. Her use of the final slangy phrase "clean up her act" invokes the stage, a character, performance. To "clean up" is also an act, the act of resistance. The behavior (that is, identity) offered by her culture is an act, a performance, often of unearned privilege, suppression, silence. The text of resistance may also be a performance, acting an identity; and identity may be action, not "natural," not unself-conscious, not a utopian vision of a whole harmonious self, but performed as a series or sequence of "aspects" of identity. The first person as subject, as "I," in this writing and the third person as subject (topic) here are both engaged, the interior person and the sociohistorical one, meeting and overlapping and diverging in the act of writing, which is where we see Rich cleaning up her "act." The "doer" is not, however, disappeared in these textual "deeds." Rather, "I" takes up the place of departure, the knowing self (she says "I know that ...") names the known.

A vivid demonstration of Rich's efforts to "clean up her act" is apparent in the changing approach she has to using the words of other women writers in her poems (identifying interpolations with italics). With their words Rich had articulated/enacted the imaginative identification with all women ("Foreword" *Blood* x) that she put forward as a definition of feminism. Recently, however, Rich has reexamined that definition, finding in it an arrogance, an unintended assumption of authority—as though all women's lives were automatically accessible to the imagination of a white North

American. In "Notes Toward a Politics of Location" (1984), Rich says that "feelings are useless without facts ... all privilege is ignorant at the core" (*Blood* 226). To "clean up her act," Rich (like all who have occupied that space) must retreat from the assumption of centrality. She writes,

> I do not any longer *believe*—my feelings do not any longer allow me to believe—that the white eye sees from the center. Yet I often find myself thinking as if I still believed that were true. Or rather, my thinking stands still. I feel in a state of arrest, as if my brain and heart were refusing to speak to each other. (*Blood* 226)

Here Rich makes herself visible in the process of revising, rearticulating, forcing more and more precision on the description of her white self. Delineating the sites of silence as body parts (brain, heart), and giving them organs of speech with which they may stay silent, Rich indicates how powerfully racism inhabits the self. By outlining the silences, or the absences of engagement, the "state of arrest," Rich's text embodies the social reality of a white woman in a white-dominated culture attempting to shift the deadlock of racist habit. The knowing self that tracks these thoughts and feelings does not speak out of the "hallucinations of self-supremacy" to which Elspeth Probyn refers (*Sexing the Self* 129). Rather, the "I" speaks from manifold points of connection and disconnection with the selves thinking and feeling.

In the prose, Rich concentrates on one or another aspect of her identity (lesbian, Jew, mother, white woman). As "I," she makes her issues and arguments grow out of immediate personal experience, and by allowing/requiring herself to engage with the various silenced or suppressed or denied parts of herself, she achieves a broad and deep personal base for her political values. The prose is often the written self as polemic, in which the self is transformed in small stages, manifesting in the writing of an individual what de Lauretis encounters in a women's tradition: "that political, theoretical, self-analyzing practice by which the relations of the subject in social reality can be rearticulated from the historical experience of women" (*Alice Doesn't* 186). Adrienne Rich's prose inscribes a textual self that is unstable, provisional, urgently self-disclosing, attentive to its own processes, and explicit in displaying them. The ethics of feminist autography, making "acts of resistance" in textual processes, are discernible everywhere in Rich's essays. But Adrienne Rich is a poet.

Poetry

"SOMETHING'S BREAKING OPEN"[9]

The "I" that appears in the poetry is not less speculative than that of the prose, but it distills and concentrates the questions and clarities of selfhood. Because its language is compressed, its images specific, and its strategies varied, Rich's poetry engages acutely the tension between presence and absence in the written self. Charles Altieri asserts that for Rich, "Poetry ... is not different from other modes of discourse *except for* the focused interrelations it emphasizes and the emotional challenges it poses" (my emphasis, Altieri 178). However, it is precisely in the poetry's "focused interrelations" and "emotional challenges" that the most vivid and intense autography takes shape.

Long before she wrote as a feminist, but after she extricated herself from "that perfection of order" that resulted in poems that she felt "were queerly limited," Rich suspected that she had "suppressed, omitted, falsified ... certain disturbing elements" ("Poetry," *ARP* 89). She describes her experience as a writer who "can no longer go to write a poem with a neat handful of materials and express those materials according to a prior plan":

> What I know I know through making poems ... the poem itself engenders new sensations, new awareness in me as it progresses ... I am getting poems that *are* experiences, that contribute to my knowledge and my emotional life even while they reflect and assimilate it. (89)

The process of writing the poem and the form it takes are both active in their effect on the maker. The poem "progresses" and Rich responds to it; yet, it is her own knowledge and feeling to which she is responding. The writing has made her self different, and the difference changes the writing.

Rich integrates her commitment to the purposefulness of writing and her experience of the immediate and material reality of life with that interiorized experience of being changed by the writing:

> Trying to construct ideas and images afresh, by staying close to concrete experience, for the purpose of alleviating a common reality that is felt to be intolerable — this seems to me fair work for the imagination. (*Blood* x)

Rich allows that "ideas and images" have a previous and ongoing existence as part of the language of the tribe, or the discourse of a community. To construct them "afresh" requires more than merely reorganizing the words, reshaping the syntax. Rich speaks of "staying close to concrete experience." In these words Rich is affirming the possibility of experience whose meaning is not already determined in/by language. The concreteness — here I take her to mean that which is not abstract, or abstracted — is physical, particular, precise, historical. To stay close to concrete experience must be to stay conscious of and feeling in one's body.

Rich makes this quality of consciousness a strategy, a method of making the language "afresh." It is the "how." The "why" — to alleviate an "intolerable" ... "common" reality — rests on another assumption: that a shared consciousness is possible, that "reality" is not constructed or felt by individuals, one by one; rather, perception and feeling and response can be held by a group. The "fair work" this task of construction makes for imagination thus rests on an entanglement and engagement of language and body, on the individual efforts of the poet, and on the common reality accessible through the writing.

In Rich's writing, "participation" in the world requires and allows her to trace the world in herself. She tells us in "North American Time" that "sometimes" she has felt the "grandiose idea" that she has been "called to engage / this field of light and darkness":

> But underneath the grandiose idea
> is the thought that what I must engage
> after the plane has raged onto the tarmac
> after climbing my old stairs, sitting down
> at my old window
> is meant to break my heart and reduce me to silence.
> (*Fact* 327)

Rich's participation in the struggle against injustice brings her a double consciousness: one she treats warily, mistrusting the exaltation she feels in the call to battle; the other is her realization that she "must engage" and that the everyday demands of the world are terribly costly. No invincible heroic figure lives in this poem. The poet is here, however, and in the last line, out of exhaustion and through the "toxic swamps, the testing-grounds," Rich writes, "and I start to speak again" (328). She will not be reduced to silence, nor will she deny the weight of her responsibility as a feminist and as a poet.

"SOURCES": SCENE OF CHOICES

In part Rich's desire to understand her own sense of mission or calling, her capacity to engage, and her commitment to speaking her "selves" in her world make up the questions that she asks in "Sources" (1981–82).[10] Rich's scrupulous historical sensibility about her transformations in language is the frame from which she takes note of herself, asking, as she has asked before, what the source of her strength is. The occasion of the poem is a visit back to a New England region she had left sixteen years before. The trip evokes a precise geographical, personal, and cultural mapping, which takes Rich back in memory, in relationships, and in her own poetry. The places, both interior and exterior, must not be glossed over, but must be examined and traveled precisely, revisited in the specific time of this journey, August 1981. The dates matter, always, to Rich. The specific dates support her resistance to the false view of poetry, that it stands outside its time, that it is eternal — an eternal form, perhaps. And when the poem from within itself fixes the date, as does "Sources," self-reflexive significance and historic fact blend.

Rich uses various forms in the twenty-three sections of the poem, including dialogues with her own and others' voices; interpolations from old poems; and prose addresses to her dead father and husband, and, in the conclusion, to the listening reader. To trace the sources of her strength, and of her self, Rich starts in the present, a particular moment in time and location:

Sixteen years.   The narrow, rough-gullied backroads
almost the same.   The farms: almost the same,
. . . .
new names, old kinds of names: Rocquette, Desmarais,
Clark, Pierce, Stone.   Gossier.   No names of mine.

The vixen I met at twilight on Route 5
south of Willoughby: long dead.   She was an omen
to me, surviving, herding her cubs
in the silvery bend of the road
in nineteen sixty-five.

Shapes of things: so much the same
they feel like eternal forms: the house and barn
. . .
Shape of queen anne's lace, with the drop of blood.
Bladder-campion veined with purple.
Multifoliate heal-all. (I, 3)

Rich takes the descriptive mapping of what she sees on this return trip and layers this writing with that of a memory sixteen years old and a poem that appeared in 1968. In "Abnegation" Rich describes driving "along the road / to a house nailed together by Scottish / Covenanters, instinct mortified," where she encountered that first vixen "at twilight on Route 5." She said then "I could be more / her sister than theirs / who chopped their way across these hills / — a chosen people" (*Fact* 91). Using her own writing as intertext both affirms the issue of looking back to an original time and undermines the notion of an origin: the earlier poem too was looking for connection, for sources. Even then Rich felt herself an alien from the Protestant Scots and the French Catholics of the northeastern United States and hungered for relationship. Now as then she is concerned with survival and omens of survival. The poem's layered history works as the poet's memory, and the sensation of "eternal forms" rests on recognition and familiarity. The repetition of "things" and "names" (even the familiarity of difference — "No names of mine") confers a kind of reassurance. The most consistent forms, passing and returning, those of the recognized plants, are named. The last line is "Multifoliate heal-all."

The "heal-all" is cast into sharp doubt and marks an abrupt shift in mood in the first line of II: "I refuse to become a seeker after cures."

There is a refusal of ontological stasis here (to "become a seeker"), in this firm declaration of resistance to an implied pressure. "Cures" evokes afflictions and a belief in an external power, and with the heal-all, the familiar names and forms are put aside, and the "unnamed," the "diffuse," are valorized:

> I refuse to become a seeker for cures.
> Everything that has ever
> helped me has come through what already
> lay stored in me. Old things, diffuse, unnamed, lie
> > strong
> across my heart.
> > This is from where
> my strength comes, even when I miss my strength
> even when it turns on me
> like a violent master. (II, 4)

Rich affirms, almost defiantly, her interior life, despite its uncertainty, sure that the "diffuse," "unnamed" things that are "stored" within her are the source of strength she needs for survival. She holds to the certainty and the comfort of mysterious "unnamed" things. The ambiguity of "across my heart," suggests both promise (to "cross my heart" is the child's vow of honor) and contradiction, as "old things" may be seen as a barrier to "heart" as well as a support. The potential of this interior strength to become a "violent master" does not disturb her assurance: "This is from where ..."

Strength, then, in the tones of a "master" may be the voice that opens III. The poem enters a dialogic mode, almost a drama between this section and the preceding one. The questioner reacts to the previous speaker as if a different voice, a different consciousness:

> *From where?*   the voice asks coldly.
> This is the voice in cold morning air
> that pierces dreams.   *From where does your strength*
> *come?*
>
> Old things...
> > *From where does your strength come, you*
> *Southern Jew?*
> *split at the root, raised in a castle of air?*
> Yes.   I expected this.   I have known for years
> the question was coming.   *From where*   (III, 5)

This poem begins the interrogation of her personal, national, cultural, political, and natural (i.e., from nature) experiences. Rich is required to answer the question so coldly asked. A past self with the voice of an old poem speaks here, and Rich, in her own "I," responds as though she hears the questions for the first time. In the earlier writing, from a poem she called "Readings of History" (1960), Rich describes herself as "Split at the root, neither Gentile nor Jew, / Yankee nor Rebel" (*Snapshots* 36).[11] Her affirmation of an inner self ("This is from where / my strength comes") is made dramatically difficult and complex by the specific naming of "you" in "you Southern Jew." The demand to know the self comes from the self, from the written self of the old poems as well as from the named selves of the split identities.

The self-reflexivity in III is made more intense and available in IV. There the self as a written presence is made explicit, and the engagement with self in and as a process in poetry is spoken:

> *With whom do you believe your lot is cast?*
> *From where does your strength come?*
>
> I think somehow, somewhere
> every poem of mine must repeat those questions
>
> which are not the same.   There is a *whom,* a *where*
> that is not chosen   that is given and sometimes
>   falsely given
>
> in the beginning we grasp whatever we can
> to survive. (IV, 6)

The opening lines of IV, italicized like the other insertions from earlier poems, appear in "The Spirit of Place" (1980, *Fact* 298). The stanza there reads, "*With whom do you believe your lot is cast?* / If there's a conscience in these hills / it hurls that question." Earlier, in "Natural Resources" (1977), the line appears as an assertion: "I have to cast my lot with those / who age after age, perversely, / with no extraordinary power, / reconstitute the world" (*Fact* 264). The recyclings of lines and questions and histories, the complex reading of them, and the rereading Rich requires in her self-referentiality, make the questions and assertions vital in the processes of rewriting. Like Rich's examination of her memories, the rewriting speaks revision. The

two questions ("from where?" and "with whom?") are linked, both
in their present context and in their presence in "every poem," even
those in which that presence is merely implicit. Rich's assertion of
the questions, even when unspoken, makes the current they carry
strong. They are not the same questions every time, and they are not
the same as each other. With whom one's lot is cast and from where
one's strength comes may have different answers, Rich implies, different sources. The realization that sometimes one is helpless, having to take what "is given," sharply contrasts with the earlier lines asserting the active choice to cast one's lot, to make an ally. The problem
of power and powerlessness enters here with the absence of choice.
As the "I" here shifts to "we" ("in the beginning we grasp whatever
we can / to survive"), the "you" addressed in the questions also shifts:
Rich is no longer speaking only to or of her self, but implicates all of
us in the process of knowing and taking responsibility for knowledge. She knows that for any reader, as for herself, immediate strategies of survival are not always enduring.

Revision, then, is the process throughout this elaborate poem. Her
need to answer those questions "from where" and "with whom" makes
the process, which is a journey backward from the present moment
of writing in search of something, not a cure, but an arrival. That is,
the process of this writing of self answers the questions demanded
by the desire to survive and to understand survival. No chronology
exists here, nor linearity. The specific sense of herself in "that dangerous place / the family home" where the child appears "backed
silent against the wall / trying to keep her eyes dry; haughty; in panic"
(XIII, 15) lives alongside another image of the child:

> The faithful drudging child
> the child at the oak desk whose penmanship,
> hard work, style will win her prizes
> becomes the woman with a mission, not to win prizes
> but to change the laws of history.
> How she gets this mission
> is not clear ... (XX, 23)

The puzzle of herself, her sense of having a "mission," or the "outra-
geous thing," "to believe one has a 'destiny' " (XV, 17), is part of the

strength Rich wishes to name. Rich wants to know or discover (or create in the writing) the process of how "she" becomes "the woman with a mission ... / to change the laws of history" (XX, 23). Her look is "the bomb that rips / the family home apart" (XIV, 16), and her perception must be understood as the explosive force transforming her from the "faithful drudging child" to the "woman with a mission."

Rich grapples with "how the boundaries of perfection / explode, leaving her cheekbone grey with smoke / a piece of her hair singed off ..." (XX, 23). The "boundaries of perfection" do not dissolve in soft mists.[12] And although what has happened is clear, how it happened is not. Rich makes a tenuous suggestion, one that frames itself as mere possibility:

> Say that she grew up in a house
> with talk of books, ideal societies —
> she is gripped by a blue, a foreign air,
> a desert absolute: dragged by the roots of her own
>   will
> into another scene of choices. (XX, 23)

With the provisionality of the word "Say," Rich shrugs at the impossibility of solid explanation. However, the person "split at the root" is linked organically to another aspect of "root" — the "roots of her own will." "Will" is ambiguous — is it the mover or the moved? There is a change here from the earlier assertion that "in the beginning we grasp whatever we can / to survive" (IV) to the hopefulness of "another scene of choices." The figure of "roots" in this poem, usually an image of fixity, stability, sources, and origins, is here mobile. Rich's other images of "roots" are also unstable. She is "split at the root" (III, 5), her father's "rootless ideology" (VI, 8) dominated her vision, and, she says, "The Jews I've felt rooted among / are those who were turned to smoke" (XVI, 18) — far from her father's "castle of air," the "smoke" allows a rootedness, grief-filled. It is the "roots of her own will" (no one else's) that force movement from the safety of the boundaries of perfection, detonate that explosive device, and leave her with her hair singed but with the possibility of choice. The "woman with a mission" is thus, in part, her own creation, as her own will drags her to a consciousness of differences, a place of responsibility. Yet that view is only a possibility, not a certainty. Possibility acts as a net cast, as imagination queries whatever energies might be accessible, and acknowledges the limitations that reside in her specific encodedness.

She wonders, "Are there spirits in me, diaspora-driven / that wanted to lodge somewhere" (IX, 11) and later returns to the question:

> And has any of this to do with how
> Mohawk or Wampanoag knew it?
>
> is the passion I connect with in this air
> trace of the original
>
> existences that knew this place
> is the region still trying to speak with them
>
> is this light a language
> the shudder of this aspen-grove a way
>
> of sending messages
> the white mind barely intercepts
>
> are signals also coming back
> from the vast diaspora
>
> of the people who kept their promises
> as a way of life? (XII, 14)

On whatever possibilities of sources exist and are considered, Rich imprints her consciousness of the limitations of the "white mind" and her awareness of her Jewishness. The word "diaspora" in "the diaspora of the stars," for example, is an original dispersal of the natural universe as well as the wanderings of peoples (XII, IX, and XXI). From the reading of photographs of "the old Ashkenazi life" and their inevitable reminder of "the place where history was meant to stop / but does not stop ... / where the pattern was meant to give way at last / but only / becomes a different pattern" (XVIII, 20), Rich moves to other patterns: "They say such things are stored / in the genetic code — / ... / a mystic biology? — // I think of the women who sailed to Palestine /.... / carrying the broken promises / of Zionism in their hearts // along with the broken promises / of communism, anarchism — " (XIX, 21). The multiple codes and crossovers of the natural world and its infinite movements, political and ethnic histories, the holocaust, the old stories, and the patterns built into her own genetic codes are laid against one another and recomposed into a new pattern in the poem, reinscribed as autography as Rich questions what might inhere in a language of selfhood.

The direct source of her Jewishness, her father, is addressed both as connection and as dislocation. Rich speaks of him: "I saw my father building / his rootless ideology // his private castle in air // in that most dangerous place, the family home / we were the chosen people" (VI, 8). Rich sees the unseeable and associates the ancient patriarchs, the God figure, and the absence of earthboundedness with her father's abstracted local kingdom, the family his subject people. Analysis is supplanted by direct address to her father in an urgent prose form that configures herself as well as him:

> For years I struggled with you: your categories, your theories, your will, the cruelty which came inextricable from your love. For years all arguments I carried on in my head were with you. I saw myself, the eldest daughter raised as a son ... the eldest daughter in a house with no son, she who must overthrow the father, take what he taught her and use it against him. All this in a castle of air, the floating world of the assimilated who know and deny they will always be aliens.
>
> After your death I met you again as the face of patriarchy, could name at last precisely the principle you embodied.... I saw the power and the arrogance of the male as your true watermark; I did not see beneath it the suffering of the Jew, the alien stamp you bore, because you had deliberately arranged that it should be invisible to me. It is only now, under a powerful, womanly lens, that I can decipher your suffering and deny no part of my own. (VII, 9)

The figures of the visible, the seen, the unseen, the mirrored, the magnified, are all the zones of helplessness or empowerment in this passage. When in the abstract dimension of theory, category, or will, she inhabits the "castle of air," and the "face" of patriarchy eludes her. Discerning what is meant to be seen and where the spaces of the invisible are marked out is to take the place of rootlessness and reinscribe it as a source. To assimilate is simultaneously to know and to deny one's connections of history, blood, earth, and community, that is, the source of one's strength. It is to cast one's lot falsely. Rich makes her mirror plain to us: "I saw myself," she repeats, and to recognize assimilation is to see the unseen in that mirror. For Rich, as one of her father's "chosen people," the terrible irony of assimilation has meant choosing isolation and alienation. Rich marks her hunger for connection to community and to family (that is, for sameness and difference from her father) in another address to him, also in prose, in which she speaks of her husband:

> But there was also the other Jew. The one you most feared ... from the wrong part of history. ... The one who said, as if he had memorized the formula, *There's nothing left now but the food and the humor.* The one who, like you, ended isolate, who had tried to move in the floating world of the assimilated who know and deny they will always be aliens. Who drove to Vermont in a rented car at dawn and shot himself. For so many years I had thought you and he were in opposition. I needed your unlikeness then; now it's your likeness that stares me in the face. There is something more than food, humor, a turn of phrase, a gesture of the hands: there is something more. (XVII, 19)

These prose passages make Rich's words to her father (and later to her husband) seem less wrought, less performed than the poetry. The directness feels loose, the form tentative. We feel that Rich is allowing us to overhear parts of these private conversations in order to emphasize how much of her subjectivity is in fact composed of connections with others and how, to speak with such intensity with her father and her husband, she exposes utterly her "impurity" as a politically committed lesbian feminist.[13]

Seen as another site of choice, the apparently abrupt shifts to prose and direct speech become intelligible. When Rich speaks to her husband (XXII, 25), she begins with explanation, almost with apology, outlining the difference between speaking with him and with her father (with whom she had "a kind of rhetoric going"). She opens,

> I have resisted this for years, writing to you as if you could hear me. ... I've had a sense of protecting your existence, not using it merely as a theme for poetry or tragic musings. ... The living, writers especially, are terrible projectionists. I hate the way they use the dead.
>
> Yet I can't finish this without speaking to you, not simply of you. You knew there was more left than food and humor ... (XXII, 25)

Rich gives a sensuous description of the food: "The deep crevices of black pumpernickle ... the sweet butter and red onions ... bowls of sour cream mixed with cut radishes, cucumber, scallions ..." (XXII, 25). Life is tasted here and enjoyed, and the terrible loss we feel in

this intimate conversation over these loved dishes makes sentimentality impossible. There is a kind of craziness in this writing to a dead
man — as though she were speaking, as though he could hear her.
She has been reluctant to reconstruct him, wishing, she explains to
him, to let "you dwell in the minds of those who have reason to miss
you, in your way or in their way, not mine" (XXII, 25). Rich asserts
the power of this writing to displace other ways of missing him, and
her comments point to the absence of this man in life and his presence in her writings. She acknowledges his link with her as a source
or a connection to the most profound aspects of her life. That she
feels compelled to "recreate" him in words now is part of her need
to "finish this."

Drawing together the parts — silenced, invisible, partly felt, partly
remembered, or dreamed — all are aspects of the answer to her question: "From where does your strength come?" She uses the dead here
to inscribe a suppressed part of her life, and thus to affirm herself.
Rich reconnects with the past and with her present need to strengthen
her own present self. She gives her reasons:

> That's why I want to speak to you now. To say: no person, trying to
> take responsibility for her or his identity, should have to be so alone.
> There must be those among whom we can sit down and weep, and still be
> counted as warriors. (I make up this strange, angry packet for you,
> threaded with love.) I think you thought there was no such place for you,
> and perhaps there was none then, and perhaps there is none now; but we
> will have to make it, we who want an end to suffering, who want to
> change the laws of history, if we are not to *give ourselves away*. (XXII, 25)

The simple directness of this seems transparent, but she makes the
dead and the living allies with the "we," and that suggests reconcilia-
tion and the realization of common struggles. Yet, the parenthesis of
self-reflexivity makes us wonder about this "strange packet" — and
feel self-conscious about overhearing these words. Nevertheless, the
message is general: those trying to take responsibility for changing
the world and for their own identities are warriors of a sort and
need comrades. Without "such a place," without making it exist, we
are likely "*to give ourselves away*." These italicized words suggest var-

ious meanings: to expose or reveal our secrets to those who wish to perpetuate the "laws of history"; to kill ourselves as her husband did; or perhaps to submit to definitions of self we have not made. The peculiar sense that they come from some unacknowledged, specific source (not, in my researches, traceable) makes the words shimmer with the possibilities of other contexts. Rich is urgent in this conversation. The lack of connection, and the requirement to make it, is now, as it was in her husband's time, a life-and-death issue.

The last poem in this section returns to her present moment, her recollection of the past and the choices she made then, and to the interior voice that speaks to her as "you" and seems to pierce dreams (see II and XXI) with its knowledge:

> Sixteen years ago I sat in this northeast kingdom
> reading Gilbert White's *Natural History*
> *of Selborne*   thinking
> I can never know this land I walk upon
> as that English priest knew his
> — a comparable piece of earth —
> rockledge   soil   insect   bird   weed   tree
>
> I will never know it so well because . . .
>
> *Because you have chosen*
> *something else: to know other things*
> *even the cities which*
> *create of this a myth*
> *Because you grew up in a castle of air*
> *disjunctured*
>
> *Because without a faith*
> > *you are faithful* (XXIII, 26)

The poem makes its circle of self-knowledge, returning to the site of returns. Rich's specific memory of reading a resource book of natural history in a place that was itself a recognized source of knowledge (the earth with its simple nouns) is part of her return to old landscapes to look for sources. By attributing the institutional power of "kingdom" and "priest" to the contained text of *Natural History*, Rich undermines that kind and condition of knowledge, that authority over a "piece of earth" which she will never know. The understanding she had sixteen years before is intelligible to her now. She can now complete the first "because ..." line. The italicized voice is firm and clear: "*Because you have chosen / something else.*" The line break makes the point of difference. The openness of the second line, "something else: to know other things," suggests the freedom that choice brings, even the freedom of a destructive environment (the cities that make a "piece of earth" a myth). The second "*Because*" is the scene of loss, not of choice—Rich will never know completely the land upon which she walks because she grew up "*in a castle of air.*" Of course, the implications are multiple: though she sits reading in a "northeast kingdom," she has no natural "castle" in that kingdom, because of her father's "*disjunctured*" relationship to the earth and to his own people. In the final explanation, Rich dissociates herself from the knowledge of the "English priest." She can never know the land "so well" because she lacks the "faith" that would grant her authority over it. The last, broken line of explanation takes a leap of logic: the condition of being "*without a faith*" as a possession, as an organizing principle of belief, does not undermine the possibility of being "faithful." She asserts the value or the possibility of fidelity for its own sake. The "faithful drudging child" is reinvoked; but this time, as the challenging, aggressive voice gives answers rather than asks questions, she appears in the full affirmation of choices, of self-acceptance.

The final section of "Sources" is unnumbered, in prose, a direct address to any person reading and, perhaps, to herself writing, though here Rich is only "I," no insightful or challenging other (speaking to Rich as "you") is present:

> I have wished I could rest among the beautiful and common weeds I can name, both here and in other tracts of the globe. But there is no finite knowing, no such rest. Innocent birds, deserts, morning-glories, point to choices, leading away from the familiar. When I speak of an end to suffering I don't mean anesthesia. I mean knowing the world, and my place in it, not in order to stare with bitterness or detachment, but as a powerful and womanly series of choices: and here I
> write the words, in their fullness:
> powerful;   womanly.
> August 1981 —
> August 1982 (27)

In the first of these poems, Rich names beautiful and common weeds, but in this poem as a writing of her life, "finite knowing" is a "rest," a "cure," and she has refused to rest on a "heal-all." Instead she reads the natural history of nature as a sign or scene of choice. The "familiar" feels safe, feels habitual, feels like forgetfulness. Rest, familiarity, and anesthesia are set against memory, choice, and desire here. The recurrence of "powerful" and "womanly" takes us back again, this time to her first address to her father: "It is only now, under a powerful, womanly lens, that I can decipher your suffering and deny no part of my own" (VII, 9). Rich footnotes that "the phrase 'an end to suffering' was evoked by a sentence in Nadine Gordimer's *Burger's Daughter*: 'No one knows where the end of suffering will begin.'" This is a complex insertion. The line first appears in XXII, in Rich's address to her dead husband, as "we who want an end to suffering, who want to change the laws of history." Its recurrence in the last piece is referential, and she explains her earlier words. Of course, the context of Gordimer's writing, the revolutionary struggle in South Africa as a fact of contemporary life, and its literary existence in a novel about a daughter's relationship to her father's expectations, make Rich's "pointing to choices" explicitly political.

The poem itself is a kind of "lens" through which she can focus her gaze, and the process of writing the poem has brought her to "now." She does not gaze with "detachment" or "bitterness," but rather engages as a knowledge and a responsibility, finding herself in a "scene of choices." We recall her location in a United States built on violence, her sense of alienation from the people who "need never ponder difference," who "kill others for being who they are / or where they are" (X, 12). In these last words, however, Rich marks the gathering place, her writing. The final line reads, "and here I write the words, in their fullness: powerful; womanly." Doubling the effect of those two words, Rich wishes to fill them with meaning accrued through the process of the poem. "Sources" insists that the epistemological basis of "knowing the world and [her] place in it" is, for Rich, inextricable from the "I" in the line, "here I write the words."

"COUNTING THE COST": THE TRACKING POEMS

"Contradictions: Tracking Poems"[14] reframes that world and that "I," as Rich in a collection of twenty-nine numbered poems presents her country, bound to a cold war, "wedged fast in history / stuck in the ice" (2, 84) and herself in it, grappling with the physical pain of crippling arthritis, worn by "this battering blunt-edged life" (1, 83). The selves written in these poems are deeply troubled. The terrific energy that sustains Rich as she composes an identity out of fragments is grim here. Difficult integrations that were enabled by conviction and discovery in earlier poems, in "Contradictions" seem rawer, more resistant to hope. The poems themselves (though it is not my intention to make a serious comparison) seem more tautly strung between direct speech (Altieri describes her aim as "to make poetic language a clear mode of discourse" [20]) and poetic distance—evoked by Rich's use of conventions (like the apostrophe). Rich layers her most intimate selves with her perceptions of the bleak and violent context of the United States. She writes her body in its joyous lovemaking—"My mouth hovers across your breasts / in the short grey winter afternoon" (3, 85)—and in its humiliating and crippling pain. She uses the words of other women (*He slammed his hand across my face and I / let him do that until I stopped letting him do it / so I'm in for life* [4, 86]) and exposes the anxieties that attend her imaginative identifications with other women. In these poems she often speaks directly to the reader, not with passionate exhortations but with warning, and in sorrow for herself as a writer and for the community of which she is part.

"Contradictions: Tracking Poems" is not the writing of despair, I think, because Rich is still speaking, still urgent in her desire for connection. Autography continues to be the site of possibility for her, whatever the dimensions of anguish she takes on. She speaks "the problem":

> The problem, unstated till now, is how
> to live in a damaged body
> in a world where pain is meant to be gagged
> uncured   un-grieved-over   The problem is
> to connect, without hysteria, the pain

of any one's body with the pain of the body's world
For it is the body's world
they are trying to destroy forever (18, 100)

Her body, "any one's body," and "the body's world" (and the world's body, we may think) are connected in consciousness of pain. To deny that pain, to gag it, is part of the same silencing that makes the destruction of the world possible.[15]

The effects of this "problem" are everywhere in "Contradictions." The issue of how to "live" with it is the question of how to take on the connections, and, indeed, of how to live with pain in one's body and in the body's world. The fact of contradictions in this struggle is the problem that Rich cautions us not to forget: "Don't let the solstice fool you" (1, 83), she warns. Even spring can be dangerous, and the seasons participate in the "stew of contradictions" (1, 83) that our lives will always be.[16] Against the "heart of cold. Bones of cold. Scalp of cold / ... / The freezing people / of a freezing nation eating / luxury food or garbage / ... / My country" (2, 84), Rich places herself with her lover, speaking to her with the heat of passion, "so hot with joy we amaze ourselves / ... / my love hot on your scent on the cusp of winter" (3, 85). This is the primary contradiction — the women's passion in the frozen waste of contemporary life. The generalized wretchedness ("frozen tongues licking") is intensified as the specific joy is juxtaposed with the italicized voices of victims of male power ("... *he kept saying I was crazy, he'd lock me up*" (4, 86). Circling closer, into the spiral of misery, Rich carries her imagination into lives that are both like and unlike her own.

Poem 5 gives us damaged women. Rich's precise identification with them, her difference from them, and her sense of a commonality that the externals hide make the written self a blurring of possibility and identity:

> She is carrying my madness   and I dread her
> avoid her when I can
> She walks along I.S. 93   howling
> in her bare feet
> She is number 6375411
> in a cellblock in Arkansas
> and I dread what she is paying for   that is mine

She has fallen asleep at last in the battered
women's safe-house   and I dread
her dreams   that I also dream
If I never become exposed or confined like this
what am I hiding
O sister of nausea   of broken ribs   of isolation
what is this freedom I protect   how is it mine

Other women carry Rich's madness, pay for indeterminate crimes, share her dreadful dreams. The common horrors are not suffered in common, and Rich is filled with "dread" of the women, the guilt, the dreams—and of her hidden self. Her question "what am I hiding" implies that if she were not hiding some part of herself she would be "exposed or confined" (a nice contradiction) like the women whose condition she dreads. Her invocation to the lost women, "O sister of nausea of broken ribs of isolation," is an ironic echo of desperate women's prayers to powerful saints and a formalizing gesture of poetic apostrophe to the muse. The most-damaged beings have the authority of experience and are a source of self-critique for Rich. The invocation extends the question, "what is this freedom I protect." To wish freedom from exposure and freedom from confinement implies the need to hide, which is another kind of confinement, and to know of that need is another kind of exposure. Rich interrogates the "freedom," not for its substance— the list of sisters ("of nausea," "of broken ribs," "of isolation") makes "freedom from" graphic—but for its relation to her. As she has thought earlier of "what she is paying for that is mine," she asks of the freedom, "how is it mine": The movement of the question is again double. If she is hiding, how is she free? And if she could bear the same afflictions as the others, or if they are suffering for her as she would be were she "exposed" or "confined," then in what way has she a right to that freedom? Possession of "freedom" and of identity here is undermined, as the conditions of life (madness, imprisonment, violence) and the stuff of selfhood cross the boundaries of individual identity. Rich's use of the conditional and of the process of being ("If I never become exposed") makes "confinement," "exposure," and "freedom" all part of possibilities to which she is vul-

nerable. Her final question ("how is it mine") is left without punctu-
ation, without closure, like all the sense of possibility and identity
aroused here.

From the attention outward for self-knowledge, Rich moves to an
odd dialogue, naming two "Adriennes" as "I." The poems numbered
"6" and "7" are an exchange of letters from "Adrienne" to "Adrienne." In the odd intimacies and absences of espistolary form, Rich
appears to foreground her processes of self-scrutiny. The first letter
has something of the tone of a big sister, the second responds to the
other's worry. To ensure that the flavor of the two "Adriennes" is apparent here, I include both poems:

> Dear Adrienne:
> > I'm calling you up tonight
> as I might call up a friend   as I might call up a ghost
> to ask what you intend to do
> with the rest of your life.   Sometimes you act
> as if you have all the time there is.
> I worry about you when I see this.
> The prime of life, old age
> aren't what they used to be;
> making a good death isn't either,
> now you can walk around the corner of a wall
> and see a light
> that has already blown your past away.
> Somewhere in Boston   beautiful literature
> is being read around the clock
> by writers   to signify
> their dislike of this.
> I hope you've got something in mind.
> I hope you have some idea
> about the rest of your life.
> > In sisterhood,
> > > Adrienne (6, 88)

> Dear Adrienne,
> > I feel signified by pain
> from my breastbone through my left shoulder down
> through my elbow into my wrist is a thread of pain
> I am typing this instead of writing by hand
> because my wrist on the right side

blooms and rushes with pain
like a neon bulb
You ask me how I'm going to live
the rest of my life
Well, nothing is predictable with pain
Did the old poets write of this?
—in its odd spaces, free,
many have sung and battled —
But I'm already living the rest of my life
not under conditions of my choosing
wired   into pain

rider on the slow train

Yours, Adrienne (7, 89)

The "I" is problematized to an extraordinary degree. The poet writes to her self (to "Adrienne") about her concerns for her; "Adrienne" then answers "Adrienne," explaining to her how she is going to live. Throughout this exchange each "I" is and is not the other, and each "Adrienne" is and is not the Adrienne whose name is on the cover and whose photo is on the back of the book. All are manifestations of "I," of self, of "Adrienne Rich" and of Adrienne Rich. These selves work together as subject functions as agent, topic, and performance. The letter/poem device *is* a device, the names used are tropes or figures, and the question-answer method is a technique. Yet, despite (or because of) the tense craftedness of these poems and their play into and with each other, autography is enacted here.

The peculiar formality of this exchange, and the mixing of forms within it — the salutation of a letter, then the contradictory assertion "I'm calling you up" — make the epistolary form clearly a formality, almost a performance. What is being performed, here, is absence. One rarely writes to a present friend, and the Adrienne who writes to Adrienne must be somehow separate/apart from her. The "I " and the "you" are thus conventionalized as self and other. But this other is the same as this self, to the extent that they share the name, and this conversation must be seen as a self that is given distinct voices (if not names), and whose distinct voices are formalized and detached from the cacophony of varied selves all speaking at once.

Following the salutation (of 6) — note the formal colon after the greeting — another kind of absence and another kind of performance are suggested. Indeed, two kinds of performance are enacted figuratively: following the opening epistolary move, the conversational gambit suggests an invocation, or a telephone call. "Adrienne" speaks: "I'm calling you up tonight" — the "you" is neither friend nor ghost but a being summoned by technological or magical conjuring. Such calls cannot be refused. The "calling up" that Adrienne in 6 is doing of some other Adrienne, one she addresses "In sisterhood," is thus both the most ordinary and the most extraordinary of events. Yet no oddity other than that of ghostliness is suggested, and the tone is concerned and detached. This "Adrienne" is sensible and cautionary, an elder sister's disembodied voice whose attention is on the other Adrienne, and whose anxiety creates "Adrienne" in her context. She worries about time passing and the need for intentions that might take one past disruptions of the old order of aesthetics and security. Only the last lines reveal some urgency. In them the issue of "what you intend to do / with the rest of your life" makes the repetition of "I hope" convey some strength of feeling.

In the answering poem/letter, "Adrienne" fixes on and is centered in the immediate, physical experience of pain. The demand for "some idea," "something in mind" to make her life make sense is met with a declaration that entangles "idea" inextricably with feeling, with body. Rich's aim here is to make that which is least visible, the reality of another's pain, apparent to us (Scarry, *Body in Pain* 7). The specific route of pain — from breast bone, through left shoulder, into wrist — is both mobile as the poem tracks it, and static, a "thread" holding the parts together, another kind of track. When Rich explains that she is typing rather than writing by hand, the thread connects the page, the words, and the individual letters of the words as the cost of forming them is brought to mind. Yet, distance is also foregrounded because of the loss of touch; the hand holding the pen is lost to us, as to Rich. Her wrist on the right side (the body a vice, left and right demarcated by distance) "blooms and rushes with pain / like a neon bulb." The organic figures ("blooms," "bulb") leading to the cold brilliant light of neon make her body both natural and mechanical.

Tracking this pain invokes contradiction, the only possible language. She is living "not under conditions of [her] choosing" — "wired into pain," the machinery of suffering holding her like a kind of hostage to her nervous system.

Survivors of serious trauma must, Felman and Laub assert, undertake a process of "*re-externalizing the event*," which can happen only when one "can articulate and *transmit* the story, literally transfer it to another outside oneself and then take it back again, inside" (*Testimony* 69). Rich's will to be heard is revealed in her splitting of self, ensuring that the "letter" she sends will be received. Thus she both transfers and reclaims her suffering: note the closing of the second "letter" — " she signs it "Yours." Rich marks the omission of pain from aesthetic practice, asking "Did the old poets speak of this?"; but she herself pushes the proprieties of the private and the internal outward, making the interior apparent, throwing the body in relief upon a screen. She is "wired into pain ... / rider on the slow train." The rhyme of "pain" and "train," the passivity of the rider, and the "train" on the tracks of these tracking poems show pain as an inexorable force in the dynamic of contradictions in which she lives.

Life, then, is not an "idea" even in a poem. The "how" of living and the doing of it collapse here into the hand typing, not writing, and it is this particularity of the body's presence that makes us feel that *this* poem, 7, is the voice of Adrienne Rich herself, whereas the other voice feels like "Adrienne," more than a mobile trope, but living on a simpler plane of language and feeling. Like Audre Lorde insisting on myriad selves, Rich here speaks of the different voices of self in their differing intensities and patterns. In both poems, Adrienne speaks to Adrienne about Adrienne, and our sense of the differences between them is informative: it is nothing so crude as the thinking self against the feeling self; rather it is a layering effect, the selves separated by the division into two poems, and also by the focus on the embodied self of 7. It is *her* life that is being scrutinized in both poems. She is the Adrienne who speaks herself.

The self who speaks as a poet is enfolded in the language of contradiction. And in the reader, too, contradiction must be tracked. Some readers, as the poems construct them (us?), take Rich as a scriptural voice, finding words for "everything"; others, the ones for whom she writes, are constructs of her desire to be understood and engaged with, not submitted to. Every reader must wish to be the one for whom she writes — her distinction is an instruction. Despite the difference she establishes between the two kinds of readers, she wishes to be seen by both:

> You who think I find words for everything,
> and you for whom I write this,
> how can I show you what I'm barely
> coming into possession of, invisible luggage
> of more than fifty years (15, 97)

Her personal possessions at last come around, leaving her feeling "obsessed, peculiar, longing" (15, 97); yet, at the same time that she becomes aware of possession, Rich admits, "It's true, these last few years I've lived / watching myself in the act of loss" (16, 98). The contradiction of gain and loss is uneasily tracked in language. Distancing herself from Elizabeth Bishop's aesthetic, she says there is "no art to this but anger" (16, 98).[17] The difficulty of showing what is gained and the rejection of artfulness in loss seem to parallel another frustration with language, with poetry:

> This valley itself: one more contradiction
> the paradise fields   the brute skyscrapers
> the pesticidal wells
>
> I have been wanting for years
> to write a poem   equal to these
> material forces
> and I have always failed
> I wasn't looking for a muse
> only a reader by whom   I could not be mistaken
> (20, 102)

The failure is in the writing and in the reader. To "write a poem equal to these / material forces" is to eliminate the possibility of a single idea taking hold. The material forces contain their contradictions. The poem too must do so, and must resist the single idea. She says, "Trapped in one idea, you can't have your feelings, / feelings are always about more than one thing" (13, 95). The desire to find a perfect reader (no misreading even possible) and the desire to write the poem "equal" to "material forces" engage the same failure. The poem-to-equal-the-material-world and the reader-to-equal-the-poem are both constructions in the peculiar overlap of words and "concrete" reality.

Rich closes these "Tracking Poems" with another articulation of difference in readers. Here I feel Rich resisting the press of expectation coming from feminist readers who have made of Rich an icon of answers, who hunger for certainty. In earlier poems, "When/Then," for example, the dialogue is with speakers repeating "Tell us" in their wish for stories about community, about "the joy / of coming to rest / among women / who will love us" (Your Native Land 47). Here, her own body is site and occasion of the poem and the lesson:

> You who think I find words for everything
> this is enough for now
> cut it short   cut loose from my words
>
> You for whom I write this
> in the night hours when the wrecked cartilage
> sifts round the mystical jointure of the bones
> when the insect of detritus crawls
> from shoulder to elbow to wristbone
> remember: the body's pain and the pain in the streets
> are not the same   but you can learn
> from the edges that blur   O you who love clear edges
> more than anything   watch the edges that blur.
> (29, 111)

The emancipation of the reader who thinks that Rich "can find words for everything" is a liberation for Rich, too. She informs, "this is enough for now" and instructs, "cut loose from my words." The readers she is addressing believe that "everything" can be named, yet Rich dreams of letters "in a language / I know to be English but cannot understand" (14, 96). Those readers cannot see more than the words, mistaking them for "everything." The reader for whom she writes "this," the one to whom she speaks when the pain moves (within) her and when the mindless cold life (the "insect of detritus") lays down pain's track, is told to "remember." "Amnesia" has been a constant presence in "Contradictions." Noticing difference, refusing to suppress, gag, or deny connections that are differences can reanimate memory, release the people "stuck fast in history" (2, 84). Rich informs, "you can learn from the edges that blur." Then she exhorts, with a rhetorical apostrophe, "O you who love clear edges / ... watch the edges that blur." The poem begins with the command "Look." It ends with "watch." To look is to see, only if the witness is able to watch those blurred edges, to track them as interior, embodied experience as well as to see the zone of the body's world. This is instruction for both the writer and the reader.

The autographics of "Sources," "Contradictions: Tracking Poems," and the essays articulate the subjectivity of blurred edges where the inner and the exterior, the past and the present are not the same, but overlap, becoming each other, or becoming indistinguishable from each other, in odd textual moments and spaces. Writing herself in her world the way a mapmaker tracks a changing landscape, Rich's poetics of subjectivity claims selfhood and relinquishes identity.

CHAPTER THREE

Kate Millett's *The Basement*:
Testimony of the Unspeakable

Kate Millett's *The Basement: Meditations on a Human Sacrifice* makes
her own feminist subjectivity present in part through the paradox
of ventriloquism, speaking in an array of frightening agencies and
voices that she has both appropriated from the real world and created
through her imaginative identification with those figures. Millett
speaks here in her "own" voice, familiar to us from her other writing
as "I," situating her particular experience in the foreground of a writing that layers the self with horror. *The Basement* is a detailed account
of the torture and murder of a sixteen-year-old girl by a woman and
a group of teenagers in Indiana in 1965. Millett's book gives us her
relationship to the story of Sylvia Likens's death. She uses photographs
of the people and the house, excerpts from magazine and newspaper
reports, transcript pages of the trial of Gertrude Baniszewski and
her followers, and the testimony of Sylvia's younger sister, Jenny, who
had been boarding with Sylvia at Gertrude's while their parents followed the carnival. And she enters the minds of the characters, speaking in their voices. It is Millett's relentless drive toward self-inscrip-

tion and self-exposure from *within* the agents of this narrative that makes her feminist reading of this crime and its "meaning" autographical. "Self" in this text pushes boundaries of fragmentation and multiplicity very close to the "terrifying slide" into psychosis that Jane Flax describes (219) as the real others—Gertrude, Sylvia, Jenny—become metonyms of Millett's interior drama, and projected figures of our own cultural scripts.

The ubiquitous discourse of female evil and guilt and female reparation and expiation internalized by the "characters" determines the logic of Sylvia's death and of Kate Millett's obsession. In order to understand how anyone with a Ph.D., a job, and books published can say, as Millett does, "I am Sylvia Likens," we must engage intimately with Millett's process of making herself (and her reader) into Sylvia and Gertrude and Jenny.[1] In this text we, as readers, are drawn and revised, written as ourselves, with the qualities and capacities of the characters. Millett makes her "reader" a flexible entity. She assumes a common culture, speaking from a cross-class position in which class markers are recognizable, but not fixed. She does not address race (is this a "white" crime?), and she seems to speak to a group of women and men having, for instance, childhood games in common, but strictly gendered roles within them. Only at times is the "we" she uses explicitly, exclusively female. Although the major figures in the "story" are female, the male reader is positioned as "actor" in the court testimony and in the imagined thoughts of the adolescent boys who helped think up tortures. Male readers, then, are offered a parallel reality to their own; they may "identify" with female terror, passivity, or rage, and hear their own cultural scripts echoed in the boys' reactions to Gertrude and Sylvia, or they may read as disassociated "outsiders."

The book speaks coolly through liberal reason and passionately in feminist insight, flatly in the language of police and court documents, and, most powerfully, in the interior (fictional) voices of the victim and her tormentors. Millett addresses us, herself, and them, and she speaks for them. She disappears her own "I," seems not to stand behind the text but to inhabit the embodied spaces of Gertrude and Sylvia, and elsewhere finds them in herself. She undoes her creations, exposing the fictions, and her understanding of the fears and desires that inform those fantasies. Millett emphasizes the distance that being a word maker places between herself (and us as readers and writers) and the people she is writing about. Yet, words were central to these people and to this horror — central to Sylvia, who had the words "I am a prostitute and proud of it" carved into her abdomen with a hot needle, and central to Gertrude, who chose them. That body and its words, re-created in this text, were real in the flesh of a young girl, and "real" as a manifestation of "the" female body inscribed with its guilt: sex. But Sylvia Likens, the coroner's report proved, was a virgin. Her crime was not sexual action, but sexuality itself, and for a female, Millett argues, in the discourse of her culture, sexuality is her self.

After the dedication to Sylvia Likens, before "Part One," *The Basement* opens with these words:

> On October twenty-sixth, 1965, in Indianapolis, Indiana, the starved body of a sixteen-year-old girl named Sylvia Likens was found in a back bedroom of Gertrude Baniszewski's house on New York Street, the corpse covered with bruises and the words "I am a prostitute and proud of it" carved upon the abdomen. Sylvia's parents had boarded her and her younger sister, Jenny Likens, with Gertrude in July. The beatings and abuse Sylvia suffered over the summer had increased so by September that the last weeks of her life were spent as a captive in the basement of the house. Gertrude Baniszewski was indicted for the murder, together with three of her teenage children and two neighborhood boys, Coy Hubbard and Richard Hobbs.

It is the first of the many repetitions of those facts, those names, those events. Millett's opening meditation, addressing Sylvia Likens, begins with an assertion of Millett's own repetitions: "In how many sad, yellow hotel rooms have I spoken to you, writing these words before me on the wall" (11). She writes of her fourteen-year "obsession" in which Sylvia Likens was a "story I told to friends ... even to strangers" since Millett's first encounter with Sylvia's story in a magazine. Millett's first gesture here is a linking one — of her self and Sylvia Likens. They "touch" with Millett's voice. Her obsession, her own circling repetitions, are established immediately. That we already know the facts does not prevent Millett from repeating, "Your body had been hideously mutilated and with the words 'I am a prostitute and proud of it' engraved upon the abdomen" (11).

The specific, personal, private, idiosyncratic notion of her obsession that Millett establishes in the first paragraph she undoes in the second: "You have been with me ever since . . . a nightmare, my own nightmare . . . of growing up a female child, of becoming a woman in a world we have lost and where we are everywhere reminded of our defeat" (11). She investigates her own relation to Sylvia Likens as figure and as independent, historical person and brings into question the textual status of Sylvia Likens: "That you endured it at the hands of a woman, the hardest thing in the fable" (11). Millett requires us to know Sylvia Likens as a dead girl in Indiana and as the representative of female children in North America, 1965 (and, with the word "fable," as the fleshly echo of an ongoing literary tradition).

For Millett the story could not at first be retold (told?) in words. She explains (addressing herself to Sylvia) that she sculpted cages, "the first series even done in a basement" (12), each cage "an oblique retelling of your story" (12). Millett's telling and retelling of this story suggest that Gertrude/Sylvia are the expression in the flesh of social hysteria—the suppression of and obsession with desire, guilt, and sex. The characters/people (both appear here) are representations of bodies with little access to language. Gertrude suffers from skin afflictions[2] and Sylvia from the cigarette burns, the scars, the words carved into her skin. And Kate Millett herself, with no access at first to words, builds cages, dozens of them, five series she tells us. Now a writer, she the focusing lens of social obsession, the same social obsession that made Sylvia Likens this victim, she speaks the forbidden desire of all who hear of such a "case": the "sick" or at least conflicted desire to know, to understand, to imagine, to feel. To suppress that desire is to deny it language, and to deny the self its mirror. Yet, this is no Sadean "fable,"[3] in which sexual suppressions find a particularly dramatic outlet.

The hysteric body of this text, inscribed compulsively in Sylvia Likens's torments and Kate Millett's identifications, is not only hysterical. In the interstices of the hysterical speech of rage, guilt, fear, and desire, *The Basement* interprets, analyzes, and integrates. It speaks with the language of the mind as well as that of the body. These languages make an autography that incorporates victim and tormentor, reader and writer, self and other in an interrogation of feminist ethics. With this fragmented mirror of the self and society, Kate Millett takes us into common places of childhood—the games, the teasing, the bullying. She recalls the tying games—the basement games of sexual experimentation—and the excitement of "the waiting in the dark" (19) for the attack, the game that "trains" women for their role as passive victim.

As Millett encircles herself, her moment of first meeting Sylvia Likens, her descriptions getting increasingly personal, specific, the personal embraces a larger being than the merely individual Kate Millett. We see Millett here as she sees herself retrospectively, reading about Sylvia Likens in *Time* magazine, sitting in the canteen at Barnard College, describing her "sick fascination," her "horror," "anger," and fear: "The fear especially, an enormous fear" (14). And the feminist consciousness (not ideological here, but intensely associative) charges the fear with a deep identification: "Because I was Sylvia Likens. She was me.... She was what 'happens' to girls. Or can. Or might ... if you are sixteen, or ever have been or female and the danger is all around you. Women, the corpses of women, surfacing in newsprint" (14). Millett's "I" becomes "you" and then "we," and the personal is exposed as public, and shared. Her assumption is that every woman will identify equally. She says, "We all have a story like this, and I had found mine" (14). The "story" here is the objective correlative for the internalized fear and shame of femaleness in our culture, and it is recognizing that story as a cultural "fable" that is the product (and producer) of a feminist consciousness. The female self/subject here, then, is both subject as agent of selfhood and subject as topic, as passive, as written upon.

Millett anticipates the frustrated, reasoned reactions to the atrocity: "you think, why the hell did they do this?" (14) and echoes an answer the reader is expected to recognize:

And then you see the line about being a prostitute and you know, though you can hardly think — in the sense of conceptualizing it — you know, it is for sex. That they killed her for sex. Because she had it. She was it. . . . Because nubile and sixteen she is sex to the world around her and that is somehow a crime. For which her killing is punishment. Execution. A sentence carried out. Upon Shame. (14)

The broken syntax here suggests that only a small piece of this knowledge can enter at one time. Millett fragments it for forcefulness, and for particularizing the extended trope of a whole system of justice in action. The paragraph ends on the capitalized "Shame," and her next assertion indicates it is the answer to the question not yet asked. "And shame? The answer to the other question — 'Why did she let them do it to her?' Sure, admittedly she was tied up the last few weeks" (15). Millett traces Sylvia's story as though reading it, as indeed she did, as we do (the authority of the text relied on, while being challenged, in the idiom of newspaper readers everywhere): "But it says here that before that she was still free" (15). Millett asks the logical questions — why did she not tell the teachers, the pastor, why did she not run away? Millett answers the questions, "It was not only the body that must have been broken, but the spirit. And that is the whole meaning of shame" (15). Millett concludes her first chapter with reference to another story: "In Kafka's Penal Colony the sentence is carried out upon the flesh, written thereon so that it will enter into the soul. Here too" (15). In this sentence "here" is multiply ambiguous. "Here," in this text, is Sylvia Likens's body repeatedly undergoing its sentence(s) of death. "Here," in Sylvia's life, was her sentence (in words and in punishments) inscribed on her flesh. "Here" in this culture is sexual shame inscribed on women's lives.

Highly mobile, Millett makes a personal identification with Sylvia Likens, she makes a literary construct, and she reiterates a "case," a journalist's task. She speculates, analyzes, interprets; she makes us (readers/the public) present; and she makes us (women) recognize ourselves as participants in the shame and the violence, and in the helplessness, of the women here. She gives us the theater of characters who are acting parts and the fiction of the language of their inner selves. All these discourses, all these idioms are informed by two terrible kinds of knowing: this horror happened/these people and events are real. And their reality is not the text's reality. This is the writing of Kate Millett's interior self—the boundaries between her identity and Sylvia Likens's and her story blurred by the common fact of femaleness. And by the consciousness of the almost absolute domination of gender as the determining "fable." The tensions between Kate Millett as she speaks herself here, Sylvia Likens (dead girl), Gertrude Baniszewski (eyes shadowed, lipless mouth in a downward curve in her photographs), and what Millett calls "my Sylvia," "my Gertrude," are the connective tissue of Millett's meditations. Acutely and consistently self-reflective, Millett is relentlessly interested in her obsession with these people, the events, the details. I am reminded of the way the horror stories of war are told and retold to answer the question, "What was it *really* like? The obscenity and intensity of the trenches and the jungle treks have become obsessive icons of manhood in western culture. Perhaps Kate Millett's is the female version of the male war story: that is, *this* story tells what it *really* means to be a man/woman.

The Basement is arranged in three segments or "parts"; each tells the same story. The movement is not chronological, but rather spirals inward, seeming to look for a center to the puzzle, to the horror and mystery, and finally even to the experience of Sylvia and Gertrude. With each turn of the spiral, Millett moves into a greater intimacy with Sylvia Likens, focusing more intently on her exhausted defeat. The first unit, Part One, is organized into numbered chapters, unlike Parts Two and Three, in which section breaks have no formal attention drawn to them. The control and organization evident in Part One seem to be straining to hold in the physical and emotional violence of this story and of Millett's passionate relation to the text she is making. In Part One, Chapter One, Millett gives us herself, her obsession; she gives a dead girl, the shocking circumstances of her death, and the conventions of a midwestern funeral. Moreover, she offers a context, social, ideological, and literary, in which this death can be understood. In fact, she insists that this murder must be understood, rather than merely dismissed as the work of "moral imbeciles." She starts from the end of Sylvia's life, which is not the end of her story.

The setting, in microcosm, is framed by Kate Millett in her hotel rooms rehearsing the words we are reading. In a sense this writing is the end of Millett's involvement with Sylvia Likens, though it is the beginning of this text. The specific beginning for Millett is fixed at the point where she comes across the story in a magazine she is scanning between classes. The layered beginning, then, is paralleled by the ending, the first layer of which opens the book. The larger frame is the ideological boundaries of this crime. These Millett textualizes as a "fable" and "emblem" of a world lost to women, in which fear and shame, guilt and punishment are linked to female sexuality. The book itself, as object, ends with an appendix of grainy black-and-white photographs of the people and things that grip Millett. It contains portraits of Sylvia Likens, Paula Baniszewski (her mouth a down-curving slash like her mother's), and Coy Hubbard in familiar school photograph format; newspaper snapshots of Gertrude Baniszewski, her children, and the large clapboard house in which they all lived; photographs of the bathroom (big clawfoot tub, dirty toilet with the seat up, and magazines littering the floor); the filthy basement stairwell (rags, paint cans, a broken chair) where Sylvia was kept; and courthouse crowds trying for a glimpse of Jenny Likens. The last photo of the series is labeled "Mother and son bid farewell. Gertrude Baniszewski embraces her son, Johnny, after sentencing, May 25, 1966." In the text, Millett gives us the photos through her relation to them: "When I write I hold them before me. Them. Gertrude and her band; even the house on New York Street, even its basement. Photographs only, of course. All I can get" (16). This opening of the second chapter again establishes Millett at the heart/center of the story, reading and rewriting the experience — holding the "characters" (with regret that it is only photographs she can get?).[4]

The photos evoke Millett's conjecture and speculation. She muses on the changes that Gertrude undergoes in the course of her imprisonment with the comfort and care and good food available in prison; with the freedom from the grind of poverty and a horde of children to feed; with her lawyers' careful choice of clothes for her. She exudes energy in the pictures. Millett considers the responses of lawyers, press, and public. Her speculations are presented as that, tentative and conversational. With the casual tone the excessive and bizarre rapidly become familiar. The alien and dreadful seem to peel back, revealing the ordinary and conventional. Millett considers Gertrude's response to the men now around her, "how their eyes seemed to respect the crime in its participants, their manners nearly courtly, 'nicer' than any she had known in men" (18). Millett's prose slips from her musing about Gertrude to the reporters: "always she was important ... Evil beyond any evil these figures had ever approached ... the big one ... Because it was torture. A thing nearly unknown. Or so common on a small scale as to be overlooked. But torture to death held almost a grandeur" (18). The angle of her attention takes another shift as her consideration of the reporters' fascination with Gertrude becomes a general imaginative invitation into the event:

> To be tied in a basement and slowly and ritually murdered. The nightmare of everyone, remembered from or first expressed in the games of children, all the endless rigamarole of ropes, knots, games of blindfolding or gags.... Even the very habit of playing in basements ... cool and damp, cavelike and hidden.... Places of sexual experiment.... Or the murder games in darkened houses.... its suspense both terrible and delirious, the waiting in the dark, a waiting almost sexual, the moment of assault, the moment played out in a hundred films. (18–19)

This evocation of the familiar and the shared is the most common of Millett's rhetorical strategies at this stage, and it lulls and quiets the reader until an abrupt shift brings us back to Millett, and the photographs, and the reality behind the photos: "But all this is a far more subtle affair than the filthy bundle of clothes under Gertrude's cellar steps" (20). Millett collapses "I" and "you" in her description of the photos and their effects. She says, "The very way of telling makes you gasp in unforeseen response," and reasserts the writtenness of this event by asserting the inadequacy of words: "shock or horror or disgust—all words so cheap and ineffective when compared to the picture or the sensation it evokes" (20). At the same moment that she disparages the power of words in contrast to the impact of the visual (which she takes as the real, imbued with ideological significance), Millett revalorizes the efficacy of language to break through the still silence of the photograph and into a narrative of recollection and fantasy. She twists the memories, inviting us into the basements of our own childhoods, then suspends those memories while the socially responsive adult carries us with her as she reacts to the photographs of the house: "The very sordidness of that staircase, the humdrum poverty of the sink makes us ashamed such human lives were ever lived" (20). With that sensibility Millett takes "us" closer to such lives: "endless tomorrows so barren of hope or even interest that they chose to kill for sustenance.// And entertainment. Because it must have been fun" (20). Millett forestalls readerly resistance by establishing a position and then reflecting on what she has asserted: "fun. Peculiar word. This takes a long time to discover or admit" (20). She allies herself with her reader's recoil against the idea of torture as fun, and thus draws us close as she tracks the insistent force of her insight: "So obvious, lying right in sight, the insistence borne in on you at last, that with whatever anger or confusion ... religious correctness ... even beyond these full satisfactions—there was pleasure. Excitement, the special excitement of group sport. Even its sense of play, of game, of improvised theatre" (20). Abruptly the common ground between the torturers and the reader (and writer) is reasserted. Millett elaborates on the kinds of "fun"—the sexual energy of all the childhood basement games and the concomitant master-slave, captor-captive relations, the sense of fantasy and power—but as she draws this familiar picture, the real events again rise against the fantasy and shared experience:

> This is the thing come true. Because the victim has no complicity ... is not a player. Because this is not play, has passed beyond that, has become life. For the victim. And for her younger sister, Jenny Likens, who was made to stand by helpless. For the tormentors it is still play, playing with their victim's life, as one animal worries the body of another to death, the moral order of human beings utterly transcended. (21)

From the generalities and abstractions Millett selects details to demonstrate the kind of fun, play, power the "basement theatre" allowed: "laughter ... as Johnny hits upon the brilliant idea of shoving Sylvia down the basement steps ... the 'good times' of group enterprise, the chumminess ... And for wit they forced Sylvia to insert a Coca-Cola bottle in her vagina. They had fun" (21).[5] Distanced by revulsion, we are drawn back again, this time by Millett's sociohistorical speculations:

"the public relished this case ... special appeal in crime ... enacting the forbidden ... always the thrill of identification" (22); and she names the inclusive categories of adults who have ever struck a child or wanted to as those who may well identify with Gertrude (22). With the constant embrace and repulsion of this chapter, Millett subverts any suspension of ambiguity in our responses. With her, we must be appalled by the horror of Sylvia's death, while we acknowledge a kind of association with the type of killing it was. The torturers are humanized by our likeness to them, while the crime is exposed in its full grotesqueness.

Millett dramatizes the moment of finding, in the five volumes of documents from the trial and newspapers, the series of photographs of Sylvia as a naked corpse, body scarred with cigarette burns, mutilated, a particular image: "But ... it was the mouth.... Looking at this mouth would drive me mad, because both lips had been chewed almost in half.... Self-inflicted. This was not done to her—but of course it was.... A grief so grievous it wounds itself" (25). Millett focuses on this wound, the torn mouth of the girl, and the double anguish of a self-inflicted torment when the self is already destroyed by others. We note the double focus, in which the text mirrors Millett's own anguish as well. Millett's intensity in the face of this particular detail mirrors her own anguish of the mouth—the seeing, and the telling. It is the "looking" that would drive her mad. It mirrors her own reliving of Sylvia's experience. Her own place of speaking is an obsessive one, the pain of the telling not simply self-inflicted but a requirement of both her personal psychological organization (this is her "story" we recall) and her feminist grasp of Sylvia as any sixteen-year-old girl in our culture.

Millett treats the court records and testimony of police, doctors, and defendants as she does the photographs: she fragments them and then reflects on, analyzes, and interprets the details. In short, she makes meaning, an epistemology of emotional and imaginative association and speculation out of her immersion in the documents of this time, these people. With the transcripts of testimony, the voices of the torturers and of Jenny Likens, Millett constructs scenes, dramatizations that make it possible and necessary to enter the events. Like her reactions to the photographs, Millett traces her responses to the legal testimony. Fixing our gaze on the photographs or the testimonies, the text moves into narrative reconstructions of how it may or must have been, how a particular event could have developed, and how it felt to be there in the body of Gertrude, of Jenny, of Sylvia in the moments in which, for example, Sylvia is held under scalding water.[6] Millett describes the photograph of the bathroom:

> Only the tub is mysterious. It has feet. The amiable old-fashioned claw kind, the claw clutching a ball, the ball resting on the floor.... An object as heavy with innocence and familiarity as a cast-iron bathtub.... Paula holding, Gertrude holding, the water hot beyond bearing, Sylvia's skin burned around the neck and shoulders as Ellis testified.... The foray as Sylvia is driven into the bath, carried, lifted, one figure at her head, one at her feet.... This took place a number of times each week. On an ordinary Friday night, Coy Hubbard [a teenage neighbor] might drop by when Sylvia would be in the bath, subjected to the bath.... The sound of it [a body] struggling as others hold it, lower it into the fierce water, the thrashing about, the pleading. All gone now. The room is empty, indifferent. Looking at the photographic copy of it, it is hard to conjure up all their legs, Paula's and Gertrude's grouped around the clawed feet. The sounds. The commotion. (59)

The peculiar focus on the legs of these people, this almost askew moment of imagination, is what makes the passage full of tension. The photographic image is peopled, invested with sound and feeling, terror and pain. The ordinary Friday-nightness of it slides into the perplexing violence and then the momentary envisioning of the legs, the commotion, charges the scene with presence at the same time instant absence (the flat black-and-white image) is evoked.

The chronology of events is utterly disrupted — a piece of factual evidence will receive glancing attention, and then the text will return to it, creating a scene, or a discourse, or a musing often from varying perspectives, until the fullest possible textualizing of the experience, of Millett's inhabiting of the experience, is achieved, until the specificity of the pain is lost in the repetitions, for the reader as it must have been for Sylvia. Virtually every violence that Sylvia Likens was subjected to is treated in this way, but some lend themselves to particular readings. Millett pays both precise and deeply associative attention to the fact that Sylvia's vagina was kicked repeatedly by

Gertrude and various others. First mention of the kick is made in the doctor's testimony: " 'The external vagina was swollen and ecchymotic as though it had been kicked—it was extremely puffy, the labia' " (36, n. 16) and to further questioning by the prosecutor:

"Doctor, you stated you examined the labia and pubic area?"
"That is right."
"Did you find any evidence of sexual manipulation?"
"No sir, I did not, or molestation." (38, n. 19)

Millett notes:

It seems curious that the kick directed to the vagina ... does not qualify as molestation, but the meaning of this exchange is narrower: there was no doing to Sylvia of a sexual nature, only of a hostile one. Just as the instrument of her rape was a Coca-Cola bottle, self-imposed because Sylvia was forced to insert it into her vagina.... sex was to hurt and humiliate, but not to partake of. And so Sylvia Likens probably died a virgin to her tormentors. And they avoided sin and contamination. Because they kicked, rather than fucked her. (38)

The use of the plain word "fucked" separates Millett irrevocably from puritanical forces and from those who can so neatly separate sexuality from the violence of a kick to the genitals. The kicking, as part of the generalized pattern of torture, is submerged, but surfaces repeatedly as Millett makes the connections explicit between this torture and others: the literary (Kurtz's skulls in *The Heart of Darkness* being horror, being "artifact" and Sylvia Likens's face in death "a product, an artifact" [42]); the political (Millett wonders if the Iranian secret police torturer has a "mental cast similar to that of Richard Hobbs? or Gertrude?" [43]); and the gendered. Inevitably, Millett is reminded of the genital mutilation of young women in various cultures, the most disturbing parallel of which is that "however much this act is the will of the tribe and its men, it is done by women" (44). Millett points out that among all the arguments supporting clitoral excision, the strongest is that against female autonomy, independent sexual pleasure. She says, "Here is ideology. And not altogether foreign to that which pressed in on Sylvia" (45). She returns to the courtroom and to another description of the testimony about the kick. "Having established that this hematoma is a bruise ... and that all this is indication of a blow to the vagina, probably a kick—'this would take a pretty good blow' [n 22], Ellis asserts in a particularly unfortunate choice of words" (50)—the prosecutor must still ask for clarification of sexual damage. Millett comments, "Girls are only damaged one way" (50). Her elaborated response to the medical evidence that "no entrance occurred" (n. 23) is sharp with indignation:

> A dry fuck indeed. A kick. But no entry by hand or mouth or tongue or penis. Sexuality without sex. Pure ideology. Ideas about sex, notions, values, superstitions, feelings, hatreds, fears—everything about sex but the thing itself, the act of it of such powerful taboo that one resorts to violence, to sadism, to any and every brutality to avoid it. To stamp it out. The doctor's voice goes on in the courtroom. (51)

The medical reports and the social attitudes they expose, these are the voices of reason and control; but later in this text Millett reconstructs the kicking, Gertrude's voice a master of ceremonies directing the group brutalities against Sylvia:

> "Your gonna get a real kick out of it too. We're gonna put the boot to you. Right between the legs. Right where the problem is. We're all gonna work on you. First I want Rickie to try. But I'm gonna show you first, Rickie. You gotta aim real good and get her right in the center.... Watch what I'm gonna do now, all of you. There, right there. See that? Listen to her yell.... You'll get your turn Paula, but I want the boys to be first. They gotta meet the devil head on. That's sin, Rickie boy, kick it hard. Hard's ya can.... That's enough, now remember it's dirty." (270–71)

This passage is typical of the last third of the volume, which is dominated by parallel monologues of Gertrude and Sylvia that finally become a kind of dialogue between them. Intermittent passages of testifiers, minor participants, and, never long silent, Millett speaking in her own voice link events by association rather than by linear time. Following the previous passage, Sylvia's voice speaks:

> "Still after they're gone, it keeps on happenin, her over me, tellin 'em how. No, I shove her outa my mind. The kickin did it. That Gertrude would stand over me and watch my face.... With Rickie and Johnny watchin so they could do it too and that big fat Paula kneelin on my legs." (271)

Later, Millett returns to the scene from the perspective of one of the teenagers present, a young man who "grinned" a lot during his testimony: "She [Gertrude] was really kind of a freak in his opinion, a loser. Sylvia, too, matter of fact. Different way, but the same thing. Most people were losers really if you watch them—and really you want to keep most of yourself clear of them" (317). Millett glides from conjectures about Randy Leper to his own voice and funnels us into the scene of Randy thinking to himself while he watches the court proceedings, assessing the other participants in the beatings, remembering various occasions at Gertrude's, (re)living those moments:

> "Lookit Gerty showin off in front of us. Grown-up woman hittin a girl with two guys watchin. Johnny wants to do it now too.... not sure his old lady's gonna let him by, doin it. Okay for her, but is it okay for him? Wouldn't mind tryin myself. Might be fun. Might be interestin. Never hit one of 'em there." (319)

The ideological substratum, the loathing of female sexuality that these brutalities reveal, is reinforced by the attention to the words used to torture Sylvia Likens. Millett returns again and again to the tattooing with a hot needle the words "I am a prostitute and proud of it" on the girl's belly. The physical branding was said to be retribution for Sylvia's alleged "branding" of Paula with a bad name at school. The collapse of metaphoric "branding" with a bad name and the physical branding of the girl's body suggests a kind of breakdown of different dimensions of reality—the physical and the verbal. Words take on magical powers here. Millett links the etching of these words with her eroticized account of the paddling that Paula administered under Gertrude's direction. Gertrude is remembering punishing Sylvia and Jenny for eating too much at the church picnic:

> Now we always count, gives suspense cause they never know how many. And they're just screaming wild now the noise comin way down in their chests, nearly chokin they're cryin and beggin and talkin and up to ten now and I can feel it in my pants. Even my stomach's excited like when you hurry it or when you're scared.... If I didn't look, if I didn't see I'd just hear the yellin and want 'em to shut up. Might even feel sorry. But it's lookin. When I see them red little butts thrash around on the bed— guess you could get as excited by touchin 'em.... But that's bad. Devil's work. Not even supposed to think about that. Lookin's different. Lookin when they bein corrected and taught not to make pigs of themselves in public.... Gotta see it. Gotta watch. Gotta look, look, look at them butts, them little asses laid out flat on the bed ... on their bellies.... Yellin so loud I worry sometimes course anyone's in the right whippin a child but

still. Never mind. Watch 'em, Paula's arm up and down and their sobbin.
Redder redder movin. Here it is, here here. Yes. Look at that red bottom
on Sylvia, few more it'd be blood. Yes. Yes. One more and I've got it.
There. Oh my god there. (207–8)

This passage occurs late in the text. The explicit eroticism, or sexual-
ization, of the early beatings is textually linked to the attribution of
sexual evil to Sylvia. Desire and punishment are implicated deeply
with each other here as the object of desire is punished and the punishment simultaneously fulfills and displaces desire, with the added
benefit of purifying the object and the agent both. That is, achieving
the desired goals, conscious and unconscious (purification through
punishment, orgasm through domination), allows the gratification
of completion while implying the necessity of repetition. Millett's
rhetoric here of fundamentalist righteousness, sadomasochistic porn-
ography, and Joycean stream of consciousness combines to make intelligible the desire and fury and lust propelling a Gertrude. Indeed,
we might wonder if the writing of arousal here is designed to make
the reader *feel* the pleasure of that sexual rhythm along with that
"lookin." The gaze is innocent, while its object is not. The sexualized
Sylvia is thus indisputably "a temptation," and one that Gertrude
has "vowed to the Lord" to chastize and "correct" (213).[7] Millett engages here in a delicate maneuver. She makes us complicit with Gertrude insofar as we share the gaze and experience her arousal. But
Millett prevents the pornographic rhetoric from functioning porn-
ographically — that is, with unmitigated erotic response — by the tim-
ing of this scene. The eroticized beatings took place early in Sylvia
and Jenny's presence in Gertrude's house, yet they appear late in the
text. By the time the reader encounters this sight of erotic "pleasure"
or arousal, possibilities have been utterly exhausted just as Sylvia's
strength has been.

With the inscription on Sylvia's body, Millett gives us a variety of
comprehensions. Randy Leper's view: "all this time they're tellin her
what a shit she is and she's sayin go to hell — but the writing did it.
She agrees with 'em now. That proved it somehow, she can't get away
from livin behind them words" (319). Gertrude, to Sylvia: " 'No one
will ever marry you now. You can't take off your clothes for no man

now ... You're proud of it, ain't you. You're proud of it Sylvia.' The sobs harder, longer, more distant, forlorn. 'Hah. Look at her, she don't give a hoot, she don't say a word.' " (286). Sylvia, in the basement, speaks:

> With whore written right across my stomach now for the whole world to see all my life forever.... So many of 'em all saying the same thing so maybe they gotta be right. And after today and the writin happened then I knew I was really what they say.... The dirty one. The whore and the harlot that they been sayin all along.... All with the guilt right on my body. Even before they wrote the words. (298–99)

Here is Millett's interpretation of the branding, of its meaning to the torturers: "The branding with words, the words themselves, were the crisis point, the orgasm that purifies because it produces disgust ... the thing that inspired it hereafter loathsome" (292). And Sylvia, kept naked or nearly naked, comes to mean nothing, "a forked animal to them. Gertrude will convert her to an ideal. And the animal is not even an animal finally but an abstraction — whore, prostitute, wickedness" (293). Ultimately, Sylvia, "the naked wretch with the writing on her stomach has lost all its treacherous appeal now, utterly safe ... named now, labeled, defused" (294–95).

Sylvia was forced to say the word "whore." From Sylvia's interior monologue: "I say whore for them. Over and over, they wanna hear it all the time. And they say it. If they say anything" (263). In this chanting of that word, humanness is emptied out, Millett insists — a kind of purity of abstraction displaces any remote human connection. To grasp how destructive this repetition of that word could be, we might contrast Sylvia's experience with that of Jacobo Timerman during his imprisonment and torture in Argentina. Timerman's torturers chanted the word "Jew" as they beat him.[8] Timerman could take on the word: he was a Jew, and inhabited that identity with pride, using their hatred for strength and affirmation and community. No such possibility could exist for Sylvia with the word "whore." With the branding, Sylvia Likens's body speaks against her in an explicit accusation, the flesh no longer merely a metaphor for guilt, but a referent for the sign it carries. When the body is so articulate, its power to communicate inwardly must be at least as powerful as the external message. The purpose (and function) of the writing, or even of the mere word "whore," is its effect in breaking through to the sexual guilt and shame that is the submerged consciousness of any female in patriarchal society.

Millett describes her encounter with a woman who spoke to her after a lecture on this book. Identifying herself as someone who knew Sylvia, who had been sixteen the year Sylvia was killed, she described what she and the other girls had felt at that time. Millett expected the young women to be angry. These are her words:

> "But it made us ashamed.... cause it was sexual, or sort of sexual, the words on her stomach, I mean. Like even the never very clear talk about the sexual part of it, that it was sexual and everybody knew it, but they didn't say it.... But it was there and it was us, too, somehow. As if she was, like dishonored, you know, and we were too in some way.... We were ashamed even though we never quite knew why, but something had spoken to us through all this, that we were pretty easy to get. Weak, vulnerable, maybe even guilty somewhere or dirty or whatever." (68–69)

Millett's polemic here must persuade. She moves instantly from this memory of Sylvia Likens's murder to the astonishing case of Richard Speck. Millett does not, at first, focus on the facts but rather on the reaction of the woman reader to those facts: "It's the impotence we feel, reading how Richard Speck, alone and unaided and without a weapon, murdered eight student nurses, one by one, going from room to room, tying and strangling them, the one next to die hearing the dying scream" (69). Millett understands this devastating passivity as the necessary requirement "to be 'feminine,'" and that means "to be already defeated in fear by ... carefully conditioned certainty that there is no point in struggling, that the moment the enemy comes, the aggressor puts a hand on the doorknob, is the moment one dies" (70). The best women can hope for, then, she says, is "not to be raped, too. Not to be tortured first. Not to suffer long. To cooperate, to assuage, to hold out the hands to be tied.... To mimic every gesture of submission even as in animals, the dog rolling on its back. Even as in women. To be 'feminine' " (70). Barely suppressed rage seethes in the rhythm and structure of these passages, the blending of factual details (the student nurses did, indeed, obediently hold out their hands for Speck to tie them) with conjecture and surmise about our reduction to bestial forms of submission.

Millett's concentration on the particular abuses, examining each variety of violence for whatever shards of meaning can be invested in or divested from it, is consistent with her attention to the specific details of everyday life in Gertrude Baniszewski's household. Millett explains, "Finally it is not even faces one studies, but artifacts. The pictures of *things*" (54). We recall that Millett sees that Sylvia's mouth has become "artifact" (42), her whole self "their thing" (293). The inversion of person into thing, meaningless in itself (or to or for itself), that took place in the process of destroying Sylvia parallels the infusion of the power of signification into the objects that inhabit this text.[9] In her description of the New York Street house, the poverty and depression that characterize it, Millett considers, for example, the spoons: "Gertrude had nine persons to feed and one spoon to do it with" (55). Millett footnotes this declaration with an aside that offers insight into how she approaches and uses available documentation. The footnote reads:

> This fact emerged unexpectedly during the trial. When you first come across it, it seems an odd little detail, tangential — but when you think about it, it speaks volumes of a way of life. Jenny finds herself explaining it to a puzzled assistant district attorney, Mrs. Wessner: "You see they shared their spoons. One would get through using it and would wash it off." ... There had been three at the beginning, but finally there was only one. (55, n. 1)

Millett circles around the question of the spoons, taking into account Gertrude's finances, her absent husband, her brutal lover who hospitalized her twice. "But still how do you get down to one spoon?" (56) — "the spoons remain a mystery" (57) to Millett as she notes that Gertrude could afford a lawyer, a doctor, and a television, "so that the question of spoons is not simply poverty, but poverty of a special kind, a kind of disorganization hard to imagine in someone responsible for nine children" (57). Of course the spoon reappears as an aspect of Sylvia's torment, when she is denied its use (252).

The spoons (we also could consider Millett's treatment of soap, or toast, or cigarettes, or pop bottles) become emblems of a particular form of disorder, invested with a significance that Naomi Schor designates a quality of "female paranoia." In her study of the aesthetics of the detail and its relation to "the feminine," she notes that "to read in detail ... is to invest the detail with a truth-bearing function, and yet ... the truth value of the detail is anything but assured. As the guarantor of meaning, the detail is ... constantly threatened by falsification and misprision" (Schor, *Reading* 7). Millett is very much a reader in this text, and as such she seems textually to turn the objects and people this way and that, each angle of attention to each detail imbued with possible meaning, yet discarded and laid aside or held suspended in the movement to the next detail. The stressed item/object/person/figure acquires a patina of significance, and with each layer of attention its power, either as an inflictor of humiliation or pain upon Sylvia Likens or as a clue to this mystery, is intensified. Millett often speaks of this story as a "mystery," giving the word its popular-fiction connotation as well as the more elevated and sacred suggestiveness that "meditations on a human sacrifice" call for. In thinking of the mystery of it all, Millett conflates herself with Sylvia entirely, asserting that "because she would die here everything held a mystery for Sylvia" (58). It is she, Millett, for whom every object and event hold a "mystery" in that house. The "truth-bearing function" of the textual detail has in actuality had its significance established in its material usefulness as an instrument of Sylvia's torture. The emotional or cultural or political significance of the detail, however, is acquired by Millett's treatment of it.

As I mentioned earlier, the last third of this book is dominated by the dialogue—or rather, the parallel monologues—of Gertrude and Sylvia, the interior language of Sylvia in the basement experiencing her own dying, and Gertrude pacing and thinking above her. The slow, repetitive registering of these minds, of Millett's infusion of personhood into them, mesmerizes, long after the reader's identification with the "characters" has been burned away by the extremes of Sylvia's pain or Gertrude's cruelty. We watch and listen and wait. There we find another part of ourselves (in Millett's mirror) with Jenny Likens, the crippled younger sister, a brace on her leg from polio, sharer of the early naked paddlings, and gradually a silent, helpless, present observer of her sister's drawn-out murder. Only after Sylvia has died, bewildered police wandering around the house, does Jenny say, "If you get me outta here I'll tell you everything" (269). Millett wonders if Jenny's courage came from her fear that with Sylvia dead, she would be next, or if at last she sensed some weakness in Gertrude's omnipotence. Jenny is

> the very common denominator we dislike most to admit. The ordinary soul in extraordinary circumstances who cannot accomplish the heroic, who tries and tries and still can't get up the nerve. Closer to all of us than we care to acknowledge. And how we hate cowardice in others, feeling it so pervasively in ourselves.... The knowing against knowing that the enemy is inside ourselves, that we are our own undoing, that at bottom, we are despicable. And therefore we cannot act—because we have not acted. (269)

All action as repetition: just as part of Gertrude's actions can be explained by repetition (she can do this because she has done this), so Jenny's passivity is explained by the absence of precedence. Again the "we" makes this writing an inscription of us all, this text a kind of everyone's story, only the circumstances are exceptional. As a cultural reflection, this text writes the reader, not in the idiosyncratic wretchednesses, but in the familiar movements of dominance and submission, sexual excitements and anxieties, the worn-smooth archetypes of political power and mythic potencies. Despite being situated in its precise location in time, space, class, economics, race, national habits, and gender orientations, this story dismantles those particular historical boundaries. The gags used on Sylvia are "medieval"; her inability to make tears (after some hours of beating and burning) is witchlike (306); Gertrude, too, is a witch figure, distorted by the loss of ancient female power,

> once the wicca, or wise woman, denigrated to the evil female of fairy tales.... A warning, a notification to females; the news of their defeat.... the great goddess no longer protects us, we must fear one another. As all must fear the female. For the male, who has changed everything, fears these old images most of all: Kali ... Ishtar, Hecate—all words to fear.... Now in the very evening of patriarchy, sacrificing the maiden with whose murder this age dawned long ago. (315–16)

Associating Gertrude with the inversion of the protection once af-
forded women by female power (at least mythically) embeds this
crime in a kind of racial memory of loss that must be enacted repeatedly. The individuals become emblematic of an ancient power struggle, and the forces working within and against them take on an impersonal and inexorable energy.

Setting the facts against this mythic dimension (itself juxtaposed
to the grit of the imaginary conversations and thoughts of Gertrude
and Sylvia), Millett draws our attention to the peculiar language of
court testimony. In that writing, Gertrude and the others have an
existence in language that may be factual but, nevertheless, is false.
The rhetoric of the courts, of the legal procedures, of the court "gram-
marian" who corrects the spoken testimony (92), falsifies the language and thus the reality of the "actors" in this drama. Millett reflects
that the language of these people as it comes from their mouths is
"ironically *false*-sounding" (her emphasis, 93). The fiction of Millett's
constructions sounds more "real" than the reality does. Kate Millett's
own "reality," however (as opposed to that of her "fraudulent" creations), is her self at work as "subject" (both topic and agent) of her
own textual procedures. No "objective" testimony interferes with the
levels of textual reality on which Millett lives. Simultaneously, Millett seems to exist *alongside* this writing. Her subjectivity appears as
potential in the lives of the other figures, as impulse to rage or defense, as the internalized cultural norm of female self-hatred. She
desires to make articulate the instability of her consciousness and
the complexity of her insight — registering differences and asserting
samenesses: these are the bases of this autography.

Millett speaks:

> I become Gertrude. I invent her, conceive her, enter into her, even into
> the long afternoons of her end, the habit of torture, its urgency, its
> privacy, the same obsession growing in me like cancer. Like a pregnancy. I
> am pregnant with Gertrude — and I am a fraud. My Gertrude never the
> real one, if there was one. For it was all secret. And remains so. Nothing
> in the courtroom or the light of day ... the humdrum rhetoric ...
> nothing there ever explains.... And too intimate unto herself for
> Gertrude ever to speak it even in the privacy of her own mind.... Only
> its edges, its details the memory of a reddened rump (and not even the

memory, merely the picture flicked for a second ...) — followed
immediately by the realization that the household is out of bread —
Jenny or Stephanie must be sent to the store. (290)

Millett as "fraud" is confessed. Her Gertrude is made of language, but
the "real" Gertrude cannot be contained or discovered in words, for
they were not her medium. The everydaynesses of domestic life, the
demands that fragment the attention of every mother, displace in Millett's understanding of Gertrude the kind of coherent self-knowledge
that Millett associates with language. Millett's movement here — to
make Gertrude, to unmake her, and then to recreate her — all this a
virtuoso performance, in the writing, not of Gertrude, or not only
of Gertrude, but of Kate Millett. The Gertrude (like the Sylvia) she
makes is a mask for Millett. And her explanation for Gertrude seems
close enough to Millett's descriptions of her own experience of obsession to be unnerving. We recall her words "I go further into fantasy, as far as delusion, even full-fledged possession, becoming Sylvia
or Gertrude as day becomes the next day." She declares,

> One does not say: "I will torture this child to death." Torture was surely
> not a word Gertrude permitted herself. . . . She was "correcting" the child,
> "disciplining." . . . All terms that she must have begun with and then lost
> sight of later. When it became secret. Secret even from herself. When it
> began to step beyond what she could explain in any familiar terms she
> understood, if not to say aloud then in the wordless flux of her mind . . .
> it became a mystery. Something she did, something that came over her,
> something that happened . . . the great tent of it coming to a form whole
> and perfect around her just as it did to Sylvia, engulfing her in misery as
> it engulfed Gertrude in a wild new forcefulness, interest, vitality.
> (290–91)

The power of the experience, and the experience of power, is allowed
to develop because no language could affect it, contain it, represent
it to Gertrude. Limited or liberated (Millett imagines) by the rhetoric
of authority to which her Christian Fundamentalism gave her access,
Gertrude's understanding of her acts is framed by her belief that the
children "are given to [her] to instruct. . . . Because that's what it is
finally . . . the will of God, the burdens" (259). Yet Millett wonders,

> Do you think in sentences and achieve Gertrude's acts? Is it not a matter
> of phrases, single words, labels like table or rope — or more likely only

sensations: tiredness, rage — pure feeling-states only which pass through
the mind? "Get her" or "little bitch" or "my back is killing me" or even
just merely the pain in the back, the stab of it. (81)

The tension at work here has its source in Millett's sense that "these
are not characters but inarticulate historical persons" (105). To make
the inarticulate articulate is necessarily to falsify, to distort, and the
only way to correct the distortion, to make the truth possible is to
admit the "fraud." In so doing, Millett writes/articulates an articulate
historical person, herself.

The textual self-consciousness, the reiterated blurring of identities
("I was Sylvia Likens. She was me" [14]) do not obscure Millett here.
She makes herself known, available in details that require us to know
her as "I." We must feel her situation as she reads the volumes of
court transcripts, for she makes herself present as/in a body. Sometimes this seems startlingly banal: she sees the photograph of Sylvia
Likens's head, her mouth, as the eight-by-ten photographs slip out
of a folder and fall to the floor. When she sees the image of the mouth
that would drive her "mad," she says, "I wished I had a cigarette" (25).
In each of the three photographs of Kate Millett that lie on my desk
she is holding a cigarette. The superficial response that she has to the
hideous image is in fact an expression of her deep addiction and need
and desire. That is Kate Millett — not merely her mind, at work in
these "meditations," but the body, the person, with her particular requirements. It is the existence of this person that Millett insists on
when she says,

> I have lived a long time with these photographs, laid over and elaborating
> the mental picture I made standing before the real house, because I have
> been Sylvia dying or Gertrude tormenting ... and have inhabited that
> place in imagination and feeling so long, I almost know the inside of that
> house. (54)

Yet she inscribes her resistance, her refusal to take her body where
her imagination lives: "The house at 3850 E. New York Street. I have
seen both the house itself and its photograph; they are different ... I
could never enter the house itself, the present house" (54). It is as
though Millett will submit her mind (imagination/emotion) to any
degree of torment, of self-knowledge, but her body she will protect

from a complete yielding to the New York Street house. (This is a point at which she is precisely *not* Sylvia Likens.) The years separating the horror from the house, the new paint job, these do not erase the "taint of what has occurred here … an aura permanent now … imbued now indelibly over the indifferent paper of police and news documents" (55). That "indifferent" writing has been written over, and the submission in the text to the obsessive power of this "story" has been interfered with by Millett's resistance to the final submission of her body to that place.

Though we are never allowed to forget that her characters' voices *are* Millett's, she submerges or blurs her particular voice and enters her self to find the others. Following one of Gertrude's interior monologues ("I'll teach her. I'll break that little face of hers"), Millett tells us, "Gertrude's screaming still echoing in my mind, but she is easier to know, to hear again in every fight one ever had. One's own bullying yell not that hard to summon" (99). Millett uses this as a contrast to the difficulty of speaking Sylvia. And standing in her own person, albeit displaced as "one" in some meditations, she addresses her trouble to Sylvia:

> But you are harder, Sylvia, the figure bowed before Gertrude is harder to be. Or is one simply more ashamed finally, not very paradoxically, to remember this, the taste of every humiliation or defeat, the moment one is so despised one despises oneself. (99–100)

The impersonal "one" is used interchangably with "I" in this passage, particular actions performed by Millett as "I" ("I read again and again"), while the questions are posited as those anyone might ask, the feelings those anyone might have. In her "conversations" with Sylvia, Millett is thus inscribing herself as well as the elusiveness of Sylvia (indeed, Sylvia's elusiveness is Millett's); finally, uncomfortably, the textual hunt for Sylvia Likens seems to parallel the obsessive need/ lust that Kate Millett's Gertrude exhibits in her desire to dominate, fix, control Sylvia. Millett says, "I read again and again the descriptions … each time more anxious to locate you somewhere in them. … Sylvia, victim and center of the whole legend — how you escape me. How I lose touch with you, becoming the others" (100). The rhetorical flourishes here (the "hows," the use of apostrophe rather than a dialogic mode of speech) seem to stretch the literary and the emotional between them, and since the puzzle Millett wants to complete is the extent of/the reason for Sylvia's "complicity," Sylvia's "resistance," her recalcitrance in the face of Millett's hunger for her is suggestive. Millett is perplexed by a statement Gertrude made when she was arrested: "Sylvia wanted something from life. But I could not find out what it was" (131, n 27), and the chilling echo of Millett's sense that Sylvia "escapes" her is in Gertrude's (that is, Millett's Gertrude) triumphant gloat, "I have her now. She's mine" (274). The problem here, for me, is in the textual hunt for, capture, and possession of Sylvia Likens. Millett's need to "locate" Sylvia in words, even in the cage of her own fantasy of Sylvia's words, to force Sylvia to speak her experience, makes an uncomfortable parallel with Millett's observation that tormentors (whether of political prisoners or Christian heretics) want "far more than 'information.' . . . They want conversions. They want belief" (83). Bodily submission and external control are not sufficient. The similarities and differences between Millett and Gertrude, Millett and Sylvia, and Millett and the reader establish the complicity of everyone in our time and place in maintaining this ideology of power.

What distances Millett from the mere will to power, or hunger for domination, is her respect for Sylvia, for the fact of her as a separate and independent being, with a life and a death of her own. Millett, despite her (exposed) frustration with Sylvia's elusiveness, constructs or evolves her knowledge of self with her acceptance of the limitations of textual power. She says to Sylvia, to the reader, and to herself:

> For sometimes I feel I know you and have been conversing with you for years. And especially now, trying to re-create your world. As if I knew it. Yet I think I know. Or perhaps merely remember — as one remembers a collective nightmare. Or I guess. Or I imagine. But the thing is — I have no certainty whatsoever. . . . How many months now I have hesitated even to write the smallest passage in your voice, to "put down" your thoughts — as if I knew what they were or had any insight into your own particular language. Fraud. The tricks of bookwriters. The glory of Faulkner's Benji. Was that he was Faulkner's Benji. But you are Sylvia. I did not make you up, you happened. And what you experienced, therefore, would be of particular validity — if we knew it. (104–5)

Elaine Scarry, writing about political torture, describes Amnesty International's attempts "to restore to each person tortured his or her voice" with a "deluge of voices speaking on behalf of, voices speaking in the voice of, the person silenced" (Scarry , *Body in Pain* 50). The effect of these voices "giving pain a place in the world" (50) parallels the impact of Millett's *Basement*. This writing of an unbounded feminist self has revealed the unspoken webbing of connections that makes Sylvia and Gertrude and Kate and the reader (male and female) participants in a culture of sexual hatred. The "particular validity" of Sylvia's actual experience can never be known, but Kate Millett's incursion into (and recreation of) those people and events explores and exposes the cultural construction of female sexuality that makes such violence possible. It is the presence in this text of Kate Millett's own self-inscription in all its variations that makes *The Basement* a work of feminist ethical autography.

CHAPTER FOUR

Patricia Williams's *Alchemy*: "my most precious property, I"

Patricia Williams's *The Alchemy of Race and Rights: diary of a law professor* performs an autographics that extends the possibilities of textual self-making into legal discourse, cultural critique, and personal mirroring. Williams intends to expose and correct the forgetting of feelings, community, and experience that characterize what "being a lawyer means." The practitioners of law, those who have made it their daily work, are trained, says Catharine MacKinnon, "to forget [their] feelings, forget [their] community," and, "if you are a woman, forget your experience" (MacKinnon, *Feminism Unmodified* 205). MacKinnon did not add, as Patricia Williams might have, "If you are African American, forget your race." Williams's insistent presence is essential to correcting that training, as the text reads Williams's life. This "reading," enacted as prose, reflects and articulates an "I" that understands itself as both a "stream of text" (16) and "beyond language" (207). These textual processes align themselves, to some degree, with Trinh T. Minh-ha's critique of a naturalized view of subjectivity:

> What is at stake is a practice of subjectivity that is still unaware of its own constituted nature ... a practice of subjectivity that is unaware of its continuous role in the production of meaning. ("Not You/Like You" 375)

Trinh's description colludes with Williams's aim to foreground subjectivity in the reading and writing of legal texts. A subjectivity that is merely constructed, however, is inadequate to the figure of selfhood that Williams presents and I will argue that *Alchemy* offers an autographics that refutes the dichotomy between essential and infinitely deferred identities.

Williams describes herself as having pushed into the "deep rabbit hole of this book" (5), evoking Alice's free fall into Wonderland, and *Alchemy* parallels that journey with its parabolic episodes, amazing creatures, dialogic drama, and dreamlike changes. But, unlike Alice, Williams is fully engaged in trying to understand her part in the production of meaning. The "deep rabbit hole of this book" is territory deliberately cut loose from the conventions of legal discourse, and Williams will go wherever that free fall takes her, from one mode of expression to another. In the process, the "I" in *Alchemy* is inhabited. Writing self, for Williams, is necessarily writing "race and rights," and I contend that it is Patricia Williams's insistent assertion of self that makes the magic of that "alchemy."

My reading, then, of Williams's *Alchemy* as autography looks to the crossover or transitional territories in which Williams conjures selfhood as she reconfigures legal discourse. My discussion covers three intersecting processes. First, I look to Williams as reader and composer of self, the interaction of inscriber and inscribed making for recombinative subjectivity that exposes some of the problematics of agency and interpellation. Williams takes up the position of reader/critic of all that which reads, interprets, and thus defines her, and reframes it in her critique of those cultural texts. In this section I look at Williams's readings of other African American women as well as herself. In the second section, I will examine *Alchemy*'s assertions and associations of subject-object relations, the seer and the seen, as these powerful figures take shape in self-making. The third section of my discussion will track the route of polar bears through Williams's text and her psyche, showing how Williams makes the wilderness home, and home a wilderness.

Williams wants to change how the laws of property, rights, and contracts are read. She interprets the texts that control, influence, and reflect U.S. culture. And she reads what writes her. From student evaluations to the contract of sale of her great-great-grandmother, Sophie, Williams examines and rewrites documents, speaking out of the bifurcations in her sense of self that they create. Williams extends her reading of the written external world of contracts and documents to the texts of street life, fashion, conversations, and television programs. Reading herself to us as she has been read by reviewers of articles, student evaluation forms, and workers in shops, Williams constructs these layers of texts and interpretation to make herself into a "bifurcated reader" (Schweickart, "Towards a Feminist Theory of Reading" 43). The feminist reader is often a writer, too, a critic whose aim in interpreting literary texts is, according to Patrocinio Schweickart, "*to change the world*" (her emphasis, 39). Resisting "immasculation,"[1] feminist readers may reshape their relationships to texts. Schweickart notes that "commitment to emancipatory *praxis* reconstitutes the subject-object relationship within a dialectical ... framework" (49). Williams's aim is precisely to reconstitute subject-object relations through her reading practice. Refusing both the agency offered by reading as a white male and the stasis inherent in the object position, Williams enacts a dialectics of reading and writing that is itself an aspect of an alchemy of emancipation.

The catalyst for alchemical reactions in this volume is Williams's voice. The reader of law, unlike the literary critic, does not enjoy the comfort of believing that without the active role of the female reader as agent of immasculation "the [masculinist] text is nothing — it is inert and harmless" (Schweickart 49). The reader of law has a less malleable text to work with. Part of Williams's project is to reintroduce the weight of the reader into the law — to show that the text of law is not only *not* "inert and harmless" and to show its effects in an intensely personal (that is, not merely legal, but social and psychological) way. Williams shows the law as language and as praxis, the shaper of everyday consciousness. The text of the law in a contract becomes the "reader," then, of the people who are named in it. By exposing the differential situations of the named, Williams reclaims some of the power of the interpreter and fulfills some of Schweickart's hopeful assertions about the possibilities in feminist reading practice: "Taking control of the reading process means taking control of one's reactions and inclinations.... a feminist reading—actually a re-reading—is a kind of therapeutic analysis" (Schweickart 50). Williams's discussion of her fears and her dreams makes her writing clearly a therapeutic process, but this therapy is not self-enclosed and this volume is not self-help. Rather, the deep links of the social traumas of racism, sexism, poverty, and individual disorders are performed textually and analyzed as legal-rights material.

Williams's first sentence addresses the reader directly as "you," and makes the first gesture in a pattern of establishing the reader's rights: "Since subject position is everything in my analysis of the law, you deserve to know that it's a bad morning. I am very depressed" (3). The contract between reader and writer is based on the principles held by the writer and established by her naming them. Making her belief cohere to her practice means making her "subject position" known. Her "subject position" here means not the abstractions of rhetorical "RaceClassGender"[2] identifications, but feelings, embodiment (sitting up in bed, eyes rolling, hair streaming). We not only "deserve to know" this, but we "should know" (4). The rhetoric here suggests that the reader has a right to know that the self being written exists as embodied and in the rhetoric: "So you should know," she says, "that this is one of those mornings when I refuse to compose myself properly" (4). Composition refers to both the writing and the comportment of the woman. This improperly composed self is in part made up of the legal text she is reading, a long passage that she quotes for us, having explained that a "redhibitory vice" is a defect in merchandise that may allow the buyer to get back some part of the purchase price.

The case in point is that of an 1835 decision in which the buyer of a slave named Kate wanted a return of his five hundred dollars, declaring the woman was crazy. The seller argued that Kate was not crazy but only stupid. The court decided that the redhibitory vice of craziness made the slave in question useless. Williams makes no direct comment on this case. Instead she describes herself in the third person, writing in her old terry bathrobe and trying to decide if she herself is "stupid or crazy" (4). The implications of a contract here, the shadows of a redhibitory vice in place in the agreement between reader and writer, are set in motion. Referring to herself in the third person ("you should know you are dealing with someone who ...") takes the relationship out of the bounds of text; she makes a sidestep, a presenting/representing of herself as she imagines she might be seen. In this slide, the past bleeds into the present, and slave law shadows the relation between reader and writer. However allied Williams is with Kate in the ironic rehibitory vice of stupidity or madness, Williams will set the terms of this contract. She is, as she tells us later, her own property. Moreover, by exposing "vices" she is ensuring that the reader makes a deal in full knowledge — that the self (in) writing and self (as) writer as part of the contract, and that the process of that self in relation to writing be known. Williams describes her strategies for coping with "moods like this":

> It helps to get it out on paper, so I sit down to write even when I'm afraid I may produce a death-poem. Sometimes I can just write fast from the heart until I'm healed. Sometimes I look at my computer keyboard and I am paralysed, inadequate — all those letters of the alphabet, full of random signification. (4)

The writing here seems to be from sources that are not all in the conscious will or controlled determination of the writer. Fear of what may be written, a "death-poem," suggests that to read one's own despair is to discover it, and thus writing is a way of knowing what one feels. Alternatively, to "write fast from the heart" suggests an unmediated, unshaped, unwilled relation to language that "heal[s]." The "uncomposed" self, on other, worse days, leaves the relationship between language and feeling/selfhood utterly fragmented, broken into such small component bits, mere letters of the alphabet, that meaning is unachievable, referentiality becomes "random," and the range of alternatives that the alphabet offers and represents leaves the writer "inadequate" and thus paralyzed. "Inadequate" implies that the self must contain sufficient matter to meet the fullness of possible signification and to make the randomness of possibility less overwhelming.

"my most precious property, I"

Williams's reiteration of herself as "property" runs through *Alchemy*, taking on layers and tones of meaning and density. As a contract lawyer, her work is deeply enmeshed in questions of ownership, agreement, documentation, possession, and rights. Agent and object, subject and object are also elements of contracts, of agreements, of intersubjectivities. In her wish to reveal "the intersubjectivity of legal constructions" (7), not by abstraction and assertion but by the creation of "a genre of legal writing" (7), Williams constructs as well a genre of self-writing that participates in the autographics I have been mapping. Williams focuses on self-as-property, her literary or textual authority determined by the nature of "property" in the history and experience of African Americans. Williams evokes the reduction in feeling that comes from seeing oneself as "mere" object, and examines the division of self by categories of possessor and possessed (as we imply when we speak of "my" body or "my" self). These familiar patterns of thought shift meaning, and different terrain must be negotiated when enslavement enters the picture. In an American context, that history is never not present. The family story Williams traces leads back to a private contract of sale and is the crossroads at which she uses the "all-encompassing private contract to examine what our social contract has become" (16). The text of that contract, describing the sale of a girl Williams believes is her great-great-grandmother, becomes part of this text (as her great-great-grandmother's history is lived out in Williams). Williams describes it as a "very simple but lawyerly document," outlining the terms of sale of "one female ... eleven years old." Two years later a county census records on "a list of one Austin Miller's personal assets," a " 'slave, female' — thirteen years old now with an eight month infant" (16).

Entering the life of this girl in her imagination, Williams asks what "self" might mean when one's body can be owned by another. What, she implies, are the implications for selfhood when that fact has been a part of one's history and an element in the construction of social reality? This question is a crucial one here, and examining its implications is an element of Williams's self-construction throughout.

To raise the issue of race and social reality in a racially mixed group, for example, is to break a negating surface of blank race/invisibility in defiance of convention. Williams quotes Shelby Steele, a black English professor: "If you are honest and frank, you may be seen as belligerent, arrogant, a trouble-maker" (126). Again, "being seen" is of primary importance, not (only) as a psychological phenomenon, but as an everyday material one, utterly shaping one's way. Silence or dissemblance is the alternative to "being seen" as an aggressor. Williams explores how the interior and the social worlds fuse; how the "self" accommodates, negotiates, and resists the mergers; and how the sense of self finds its way into language.

The narrative makes a place for the reader to enter each of the sites that Williams herself occupies as she renegotiates textually the experience that she describes. While shopping, for example, Williams is made part of a social dynamic that reconstructs her, one that she participates in, despite her revulsion at the scene. A young white clerk and her friends, cheery and friendly, are making jokes among themselves about "Jewish princesses" when another, very similar group of young white women and men come into the shop. Designating the newcomers as Jews, the clerk and her friends make covert remarks that Williams is seemingly invited to hear. Williams says, "Their anti-Semitism was smiling, open, casually jocular, and only slightly conspiratorial or secretive" (128). Silent in this situation, Williams analyzes the "thrill" of being in the position of an "insider," though that means she has been "designated safe" and "designated as someone who didn't matter" (128). Realizing how insulting their assumption of her silence was, Williams still must understand *why* she kept silent and how the silencing worked on her: "by their designation of me as 'not-Jewish' they made property of me, as they made wilderness of the others. I became colonized as their others were made enemies" (128). Williams has emphasized how alike the two groups were: identical in dress, accent, and mode. The "othering" occurred by designation, and no territory in the social context could be left undesignated. From the position of cultural and racial assumption of agency, of the power to designate or to name, the categories of insider and outsider are ready to hand.

The self colonized by their assumptions was not, however, completely consumed. Williams says,

> I left a small piece of myself on the outside, beyond the rim of their circle, with those others on the other side of the store; as they made fun of the others, they also made light of me; I was watching myself be made fun of. In this way I transformed myself into the third person; I undermined the security of my most precious property, I. (128)

The "most precious property" is not made into an object, which would have been indicated if she had used "me" rather than "I." By using "I," Williams makes property not only that which is owned, but that which can be recognized as a quality or characteristic — "I" then becomes a quality of subjectivity/selfhood as well as its signifier.

The specific moments of the situation in the store give way to the generalized constancy of the feelings that attend this event. The "impermissible danger" of her emotions, and her cognizance of what is being done, to whom, and how, "floats," not necessarily anchored, ready to boil over (128). Having the feeling and containing it are both parts of the exhaustion. But the splitting of selves seems to be the most destructive effect. She says,

> The dilemma — and the distance between the "I" on this side of the store and the "me" that is "them" [the designated others] on the other side of the store — is marked by an emptiness in myself. Frequently such emptiness is reiterated by a hole in language, a gap in the law, or a chasm of fear. (129)

She names her self-abandonment "an emptiness in my self" — the absence of her own sense of presence (the presence of emptiness is not indicated as an absence unless consciousness, here text, registers it as such) indicating a lack of agency, integrity, or will to act. What is desired is inclusion, though the terms are not her own (128–29), and that engages her complicity. It is, she says, "a form of fear": "I am afraid of being alien and suspect" (129). The polarity is perfectly suited for the needs of the master — and the old dichotomies between the sexes and the races will line up in familiar categories — not least of which is the will-lessness of women in the realm of body. Williams implies these when she finds herself unable to speak, unable (in effect) to resist being named as "us" or as "them." She is, in part, colonized/

territorialized by her own silence. The absence of voice, of claiming, here, a space, leaves a space/emptiness, and that space (left in the self) "marks" other gaps or holes. A mark is usually a presence. This one is an eloquent emptiness, and a repetitive one, for it reiterates and "is reiterated by" other emptiness: a hole in language, a gap in the law. "Fear," however, takes up a different mode. The gap or hole is not *in* fear, but is rather made up *of* fear, and the distance is not a mere hole, it is a "chasm." The "chasm of fear," then, reiterates the emptiness in the space between the "I" and the "me": subjective and objective case. When Williams refers to her "I" as her "most precious property," she is speaking of something about which she holds herself responsible, sustaining that sense of herself syntactically/rhetorically in the active voice — "I was watching myself . . ." — and situationally in the passive. By being a bifurcated self, a self-watcher (it is the subject who sees, the object who is seen, she says later), and not a speaker/ actor in that place, she makes herself into an agent on another level: "I transformed . . . ," "I undermined . . . ," and "I gave much power to the wilderness of strangers" (128). If both the assumption that she was either anti-Semitic or irrelevant and her own silence "made property of [her] . . . colonized [her]," Williams will not allow that to be the whole truth. She says, "I gave much power to the wilderness of strangers, some few of whom I would feel as reflections of my lost property by being able to snare them in the strong beartraps of my own familiarizing labels" (128). I think she is suggesting here that identifying "me" as "them" bases a kind of silent allegiance with the anti-Semitic teenagers on her *own* designations of who is "other," her own "lost property" of self. As "strangers" getting snared in "beartraps" of "familiarizing labels," the designated Jews reflect her "lost property" and signal her submission to the familiar. For Williams, bears figure as powerful icons of subconscious energy. A beartrap, then, is deadly dangerous, for it imprisons that energy.

Passivity is not simply nonaction. It is also choice, and its reasons must be understood. The way that that split self, full and emptied, can be recomposed as text is critical in Williams's explication of "I" as a property that, though precious, may be (and certainly will be) written in the tensions between fragmentations and divisions that can, and must, be named. It seems essential that the splits are named as iterating the edgings of an "emptiness." The spatialized multiple selfhood means then that selves do not experientially occupy the same emotional, ethical, intellectual place, and by taking up space "else-where" (the other side of the store) they leave a vacancy, a "distance" that can be measured and filled.

The racist and sexist divisions between self and other (other as enemy, other as colonized territory) also reiterate self in other, and other in self: repression translates smoothly into oppression. Williams makes the leap across the gap this way:

> I think that the hard work of a nonracist sensibility is the boundary crossing, from safe circle into wilderness: the testing of boundary, the consecration of sacrilege. It is the willingness to spoil a good party and break an encompassing circle, to travel from the safe to the unsafe. The transgression is dizzyingly intense, a reminder of what it is to be alive. It is a sinful pleasure, this willing transgression of a line, which takes one into new awareness, a secret, lonely, and tabooed world — to survive the transgression is terrifyingly addictive. To know that everything has changed and yet that nothing has changed; and in leaping the chasm of this impossible division of self, a discovery of the self surviving, still well, still strong, and as a curious consequence, renewed. (129–30)

The personal, the social, and the political are all necessary discourses helping to make the leap over "the chasm of this impossible division of self": the intensive tracking through which the text moves reminds us that all senses of self are territorialized (my body, my feelings, my self), and are involved with the reference points of location in which the internal and external not only lose distinctiveness from each other, they also reassert it. That is the source of Williams's consciousness of self-as-property, to be claimed, inhabited, fought for, or, potentially as a black woman, to be lost, stolen, colonized. The predations of racism and sexism are apparent in the "safe circles" of convention.

to break an encompassing circle

The possibility of "self-knowledge" engages uneasily with a postmod-ernist view of a subjectivity that exists only in shifting subject posi-tions. Williams claims "self" as a possession, as the possibility of knowledge within the deeply felt and articulated complexity of un-stable meaning. Williams embodies her argument for a self that carries the rights and responsibilities of presence-in-the-world in her moth-er's reading of their family history. Letting her daughter know that she need not be intimidated by Harvard Law School, Mrs. Williams says, " 'The Millers were lawyers, so you have it in your blood' " (216). Williams retells the story of Sophie, her great-great-grandmother, raped and impregnated by the important lawyer Austin Miller, and deconstructs her mother's message. Williams recognizes the invita-tion to "reclaim that part of [her] heritage from which [she] had been disinherited" to give her "strength and confidence" in the white-dominated law school. But to claim the part of herself "that was the dispossessor of another part of [her]self" meant, says Williams, that "she was asking me to deny that disenfranchised little-black-girl" (217). The "profoundly troubling paradox" of claiming both the white and the masculine self ("hard edged, proficient, and western," "com-petent," "cool rather than despairing" [217]) means hiding somehow the "lonely, black, defiled-female part" of her, and her mother's, self-hood. Williams makes that paradox clearly part of the "constructed" overdetermined social sensibility, a part of selfhood implicated in the true complexity of Williams's belief that "self-possession in the full sense of that expression is the companion to self-knowledge" (217). While these terms ("self-possession," "self-knowledge") seem to hypostatize the concepts of subject position that Williams is laying out for the reader, the text itself shifts tones, focus, and modes of ex-pression so rapidly, so fluidly, that a fixed viewer, possessor, knower of "self" is consistently destabilized. Yet, that instability does not provoke surrender of whole-heartedness or the hope for self-containment.

Her sympathetic and perplexed meditations on the situation faced by a young male-to-female transsexual student (neither male nor fe-male students wanted to share bathroom facilities with her) include the following comment:

> Devoured by others, she carved and shaped herself to be definitionally acceptable.... She had not learned what society's tricksters and dark fringes have had to learn in order to survive: to invert, to stretch, meaning rather than oneself. (123)

One of the "meanings" that African Americans have stretched, Williams explores in her discussion of "will." Williams compares slave law to bourgeois notions of selfhood. The fragmenting of human qualities among racial (and sexual) lines required pure will to be pure white and necessitated the polar conception of "black (or brown or red) anti-will" (219). The "master's" nature is assigned the condition of pure will, self-assertion, agency, reason, and desire filtered through the lens of choice, in contrast to the absence of will in the slave (221).[3] Within the context and authority of that system of thought in its present manifestation, Williams argues, will is the precondition of "wisdom, control, and aesthetic beauty," characteristics of the "whole white personality" (221). She insists that "the greatest challenge is to allow the full truth of partializing social constructions to be felt for their overwhelming reality" (221). To take on the meaning is to take on the reality, and that, for Williams, is to move from the abstract and the general to the very particular:

> I must assume, not just as history [in her research on slave law] but as an ongoing psychological force, that irrationality, lack of control, and ugliness signify not just the whole slave personality, not just the whole black personality, but me. (221)

To resist the totalized construct of partialized selfhood, Williams has got to allow "whole" selfhood to exist conceptually. To reverse the simple symmetry of purity will never change the "personality splintering" of a bourgeois worldview (221). The "me" that Williams draws out as signified by that schizophrenic worldview becomes the "me" of everyone whose survival depends on knowing that the abstract designations of value and meaning leak into one's being, and the demeaning division of self against self must and can be transformed into a subjectivity that enacts will for its own purposes.

The problematics of will as an element of agency and selfhood appear in the drain of resisting racist inscription. Williams explains that to see is "to insist on the right to [her] presence" (222) but that "fullness of vision" often requires her to see that she is not seen. That recognition (seeing that one is not seen) is "the permanent turning-away point for most blacks" (222). Williams takes up that "greatest challenge" (of facing the overwhelming reality):

> To look is ... to make myself vulnerable; yet not to look is to neutralize the
> part of myself that is vulnerable.... Without that directness of vision, I
> am afraid I shall will my own blindness, disinherit my own creativity, and
> sterilize my own perspective of its embattled, passionate insight. (223)

To choose blindness, disinheritance, and sterility is one of the "free-
doms" open to will. The alternative choice makes will live alongside vulnerability, passion, and struggle. Reason and rationality here are the allies
of passion, creativity, and life force. They are part of the wholeness of self
and self-assertion that Williams reclaims from partialized constructions.

Edward Said, speaking of exiles, says that as an exile "you must leave
the modest refuge provided by subjectivity" ("Reflections on Exile,"
359). Said's view of subjectivity as refuge parallels the argument bell
hooks makes in her discussion of postmodernity and blackness. Ar-
guing that critiques of essentialism and identity may coexist with respect for the "specific history and experience of African-Americans,"
hooks says, "There is a radical difference between a repudiation of
the idea that there is a black 'essence' and recognition of the way black
identity has been specifically constituted in the experience of exile
and struggle" (*Yearning* 29). Like Said, hooks sees in the rigid grasp
upon fixed identity a wish for safety in an unsafe world, a certainty
for those who may be exiles even in the land of their birth. And, like
Said and hooks, Williams sees the "modest refuge of subjectivity" as
a place to be reexamined in the light of a desire for connection and
change as well as for shelter and defense. The "modest refuge" of a
subjectivity based in a single perspective that must be sacrificed is
supplanted not by a transcendent vision, untouched by the "objective"
view, but by the exposed, vulnerable spaces of being "out there." For
Williams to describe the "hard work of a nonracist sensibility" is to
inscribe her own struggle, to graph her own self and self-divisions
as exemplary of that perspective that "we" (130) need to acquire.
She makes her final allegiances in this section explicit: "It is this perspective, the ambivalent, multivalent way of seeing, that is at the core
of what is called critical theory, feminist theory, and much of the minority critique of law" (130). Her speaking this antiracist sensibility
fills the hole in language she identifies, and her speaking seems to
bridge the "chasm of fear" that kept her divided against herself. It is

self that is written here, and that self (and all selves?) is the cauldron of necessary alchemical change. It is this text, then, that fills the hole in language, as the emptiness in self is inhabited.

The writing, like the self, as the self, alongside the self, must be intensely personal, "highly particular," Williams insists (93). She observes that "impersonal" writing, by denying self, empowers "beyond the self" and generates "certain obeisance to the sleekness of a product that has been skinned of its personalized complication" (92). While this "skinned," or de-raced, or whitened, writing has distinct effects that may be desired, especially in constructing a reading community, she says, "in a world of real others, the cost of such exclusive forms of discourse is empowerment at the expense of one's relation to those others" (92–93). Williams insists that the "personal" is where "our most idealistic and our deadliest politics are lodged, and are revealed" (93). Williams makes textual style or mode of expression a crucial dimension of her "transgression" of convention, her own willingness "to break an encompassing circle," whether by inserting the personal into legal discourse, or social critique and legal language into a "diary." The personal, then, this new mode of legal writing, identifies, she says, "the specifics of my pain. What causes it, what sustains it, what interferes with my ability to be most fully and productively myself. My unhappiness ... makes me inefficient. It makes me hide myself" (94). A boundary between the personal and the private may be inferred here. The social construction of "self" is experienced as personal, but as the personal is also a social phenomenon, it cannot be sheltered within the world either of the monadic subject or of the private self. To "hide" self is to submit to internal interference. In tracing the tensions between subjectivity as refuge or hiding place and subjectivity as a site of personal/political links, as the territory to be claimed, and the property to be cherished, Williams makes a striking distinction: in the context of her questioning how "we may all give more power to the voices that racism suppresses," Williams says,

> I think: my raciality is socially constructed, and I experience it as such. I feel my blackself as an eddy of conflicted meanings—and meaninglessness—

in which my self can get lost, in which agency and consent are tumbled in constant motion. (168)

Williams is negotiating terrain that bell hooks approaches from another direction. Hooks says,

> Considering that it is as subject one comes to voice, then the postmodernist focus on the critique of identity appears at first glance to threaten and close down the possibility that this discourse and practice will allow those who have suffered the crippling effects of colonization and domination to gain and regain a hearing. (*Yearning* 28)

Refusing to ally herself either with a potentially racist essentialism that wishes to embrace a specific concept of "black identity" or with the completely decentered subject and the ultimate erasure of the category of selfhood that deconstructive thought leads toward, hooks moves between the two. Neither hooks nor Williams accepts the easy jettisoning of selfhood, of identity, of centeredness as experienced personally and as conceptually useful in black feminist analysis yet both authors find the critique of the subject useful for "African-Americans concerned with reformulating outmoded notions of identity" (*Yearning* 28). Hooks draws alongside Williams in her assertion that "we have too long had imposed upon us from both the outside and the inside a narrow, constricting notion of blackness" (28). The "static overdetermined identity within mass culture and mass consciousness" (28) is surely one of the elements set in motion by Williams's sense of her "black-self as an eddy of conflicted meanings and meaninglessness—in which agency and consent are tumbled in constant motion" (*Alchemy* 168). Williams's closely tracked feeling and analysis demonstrate that the distinction between "agency and consent" can be lost, and that affirmation and complicity can be conflicted and contradictory. When no clear line defines what has been "given"—when no map indicates how the boundaries of the "overdetermined static identity" can be recognized—only the testing of boundary, the "willing transgression of a line" (129), offers "new awareness," and thus leads to "a discovery of the self surviving" (129–30). Williams makes it perfectly plain that the condition of renewal is temporary, recurring, not stable: "Each day is new labour" (130). Renewal must be renewed.

"her shape, his hand"

I have noted that, for Williams, "self" grapples within the tension of seeing and being seen; that self lives mutably in subject and object space; that being seen shapes the seer; and that the "I" that is "my self" in Williams's text is not just the seen and the seer but is inevitably and persistently in process: "I" is a way of seeing (self). What particularly interests me here is Williams's specific articulation of *how* being seen affects and effects her. She says, "if being is seeing for the subject, then being seen is the precise measure of existence for the object" (28). A social being negotiates the dialectics of self-envisioning, the world mirroring (in part) self, self mirroring "the world": if being seen is the measure of the object, when the "object" is malleable, a person, the shaping power of the seer, accrues great significance. One of the "seen" places is the figure Williams makes of the visible/invisible place of black women.

Racism, sexism, and child abuse, Williams says, make a "massive external intrusion into [the] psyche ... to keep the self from ever fully seeing itself" (63). Self seeing self: the "true self, in one's own experiential knowledge" (63) cannot be trusted when the "self's power resides in another" (63). This may appear to be the familiar reiteration of the double consciousness that W. E. B. Du Bois articulated: "this sense of always looking at one's self through the eyes of others" (*Souls of Black Folk* 16). Although this double vision is often constructed or understood as a negative effect of racism, Williams is interested in her inscription of a self that is separable from self, self functioning as *both* subject and object. In this vision, self is not split from self in an adversarial or alienated tension, situated in "the degradation of being divided against [one's] self" (120). Williams challenges a conception of self that is colonized by language into a being split *against* itself. She refutes the absolute authority of words in the observation that we can "mistake the words for ourselves" (120). Here language (the words) becomes part of the specular, an aspect of the "seen" that objectifies her, and displaces the voice that subjectifies her. Williams composes a self that sees self, a distinction implying difference, and for Williams difference need not imply "againstness," but profound self-possession, cherishing, self-naming.

In recognizing the cost to her of "society's constant construction of [her] blackness" (168), she says, "Somewhere at the center, my heart gets lost" (168). The image of the absent middle, the silenced agent, is again invoked; this time the "heart," metonym of life's blood, signifying courage and capacity to love, is what lives at the center. From the site of the "lost heart" comes, she says, "a tragically powerful embodiment of my ambiguous, tenuous, social positioning: the case of Tawana Brawley" (169). Williams reiterates the confusing and frenzied media and legal chaos surrounding the brutal violation of a fifteen-year-old black girl who had been found in a garbage bag after a four-day search, covered with dog excrement and cigarette burns, " 'KKK' and 'Nigger' ... inscribed on her torso" (169).[4]

The media texts, the body inscriptions, the rewriting of events and facts, the power maneuvers by the white and black men who surrounded the Brawley family, and the rehearsal of racial and sexual hatred released by and directed at the image of the brutalized girl reflected something about the social reality of all black women. Unlike Kate Millett, who asserts "I was Sylvia Likens," Williams does not say "I was Tawana Brawley." The "*case* of Tawana Brawley" (my emphasis) is, however, the "precise embodiment" of her own "social positioning." Williams's declaration indicates the degree to which the overwritten social reality seems designed to make the unspeakable available for racist and misogynist public expression.

Williams's rage burns through the multiple and contradictory representations of the girl. The obvious truth, despite the unlocatable specific details, the legal muddles, and the highly suspect conduct of the authorities, is that Tawana Brawley "has been the victim of some unspeakable crime" (169). The relentless violence of the media and the public's attention, and the circumstances of silence that quickly surrounded Tawana Brawley herself are apparent in two of the photos that Williams describes: in the first police evidence photos, the girl, "her body so open and public; her eyes closed" (176), is seen, not seeing — in the absolute position of the objectified. Williams extends Tawana Brawley's "terrible story," seeing "every black woman's worst fears and experiences wrapped into it" (174). Williams points to the question asked by a mainstream, white editorial writer: " 'After Tawana Brawley, who will believe the next black woman who says she was raped by white men?' " (174). The stereotypes of racial and sexual hatred find full orchestration in the "case" of the raped girl whose "nature" makes rape impossible: "How," asks Williams in deep grief and outrage, "can such a one be raped?" (175). The self that Williams writes here carries its passionate refusal of that lie, and in speaking again and again of Tawana Brawley's silence, her being a "shape, a hollow, an emptiness at the center" (175) of that story, the text echoes both her own struggle with emptiness and the image of Williams's great-great-grandmother under the control of the slave master: "I see her shape and his hand in the vast networking of our society, and in the evils and oversights that plague our lives and laws.... // I look for her shape and his hand" (19). Finally Williams is left with, and leaves us with, the image of the silenced girl, lips firmly pressed together. The double bind, and the "precise embodiment" of her own circumstance that Williams struggles with here, is the terrible alternative she feels in Tawana Brawley's situation: "There are no other options than hiding or exposing. There is danger everywhere for her, no shelter, no protection.... no stable place to testify and be heard" (176).

That this cruel alternative speaks also for Williams (at least some of the time) is strongly suggested in her presentation of herself as text: that is, her shaping of her own texts in her own ways is crucial in Williams's insistent negotiations of a place and a voice. Her writing becomes a kind of testimony, and the anxiety she reveals indicates how elusive a "stable place" is. From her afternoon "menagerie of nightmares" (181), watching television and worrying that she is "going crazy," (182) she writes:

> I edit myself as I sit before the television. I hold myself tightly and never spill into the world that hates brown spills. I'm afraid that everything I am will pour out onto the ground and be absorbed without a word. I may disappear. So I hold onto myself because I still have much left to say. (183)

The will here is toward self-possession, achieved by self-containment, manifested by controlling her own speech. To "edit" herself is for Williams not only to constrain and guard her voice, protecting herself by silence; it is also to ensure that she will not, by speaking too openly, too loosely, disappear "without a word." Silence, then, when self-imposed, enables speech. Too many words, too freely spoken, a "spill" from a brown woman, Williams knows, will result in utter erasure.

Judge Maxine Thomas provides another embodiment of that other terrifying possibility, as her speech spills out of her and over Williams's pages in bubbling, flowing song, rhyme, story, while Williams reiterates the many words spilling *over* her and into her. Looking into her mirror, Williams imagines herself into the person of Maxine Thomas, brilliantly successful black judge, found curled up on the floor of her office. As Williams figures her we see Judge Thomas:

> She lay huddled in a wilderness of meaning, lost, a speechless child again, her accommodative language heard as babble, the legacy of KKK and Nigger spilling from her heart, words and explanations seeping from her. (196–97)

These are the words of race hatred that Tawana Brawley has had cut into her body. And like the stories of the raped and tortured girl, the stories surrounding Judge Thomas reveal for Williams the contradictions that worked to destroy her. Thomas's job, says Williams, was to "wear all the contradictions" (196). Williams herself, composing herself in the mirror as she dresses for work, is careful "not to wear all [her] contradictions at the same time. I pick and choose among them; like jewelry, I hunt for this set of expectations that will go best with that obligation" (196). She chants a litany of gendered racial and class necessities: "I buff my nails paving the way for my race. I comb my hair in the spirit of pulling myself up by my bootstraps" (196). Williams concludes this reflection of her reflection with the ominous and ambiguous assertion: "I am just this close" (196). She has at various times referred to her feeling of craziness, her schizophrenia, her fear of madness.[5] Her reading of Maxine Thomas is so intimate, the lyricism and the return to ancient powers so lovely, that Williams's almost longing for this freedom shadows the words she puts in Thomas's mouth. Like Ophelia, and like the root workers of another place, Judge Thomas "was singing her small songs, magic words, soothsayings of comfort and the inky juice of cuttlefish. She was singing the songs of meadow saffron and of arbor vitae, of eel serum, and marking nut, snowberry, rue-bitterwort, and yew" (197). Having "swallowed all the stories" (196), Maxine Thomas was left without her own story, her words disappearing without a trace (except those Williams gives her) as Williams fears her own will if she does not contain herself. That Maxine Thomas lies "huddled in a wilderness of meanings" makes her indeed "just this close" to Patricia Williams's insistent propagation of meanings throughout *Alchemy*. Indeed, the thrust of the whole piece is toward that multiplicity of meanings, and against the simple, the uncontradicted, solution. When the contradictions all must be worn at once, however, when the meanings propagate without meaning, a wilderness opens up from which return is impossible.

"Wilderness—a world beyond difference"

The "wilderness" is for Williams a complex territory, an unterritorialized territory. It is a consistent, powerful resource, not a space to be colonized by rationality, or even by language, though it may be the wellspring of some kinds of language; it is a construct in part, but has its own reality as well as that shaped by Williams. The "unconscious" may be an easy label for this construct, but Williams works to make the figures that come to her from the wilderness not so easily mere outlines of repression. The presences marking wilderness are polar bears. The bears are figures on many levels of reality, including newspaper articles about polar bears in zoos. The entrance of polar bears into her conversation with her sister is one example of the kinds of engagement she has with the creatures, and suggests one of the ways the figures of these creatures work for her. She tells her sister, "Sometimes I worry that I'm crazy" (204), and as she speaks she is terrified to hear her mother's voice coming from her mouth. Merging and loss of personally embodied space ("my hands," she says, "have become her hands") feel to Williams like "drowning" (205).

Her sister speaks the words that act as a lifeline, telling her to "know that all prior and contemporaneous voices are extrinsic," but these words, too, lose their inviolable firmness. Her sister speaks:

> "Cultivate the ability to seize the moment, without which ability the moment will be past and you will find yourself extrinsic. By demarcating clearly the boundaries between you and extrinction, you will find yourself on the path to autonomy."
>
> (*Extrinction*? I ask, turning inside to the bears for explication. Yes says an old bear quietly; we are closer to extinction every day. No, no, I protest. Not extinct — extrinct! But the old bear was already fading fast ...). (205)

Subverting the clear, comforting, and rational words of advice and help, words that are designed to resist the interference of others as intrusive presences within the boundaries of self, Williams's text shifts dramatically into immediate conversation with precisely one of those voices, one of those figures. The discourse of sensible self-help is subverted from within, too, as the words will not stay in place: extrinsic becomes "extrinction," and being extinct and being outside the boundaries of self collapse into each other. The polar bear figure, here made appealing, is "old" and speaks "quietly," and the threat of his loss is enacted in the text: he is "fading fast" as the sentence itself fades out.

Although some of this textual play may be seen as whimsical performance of her fantasy life, I think Williams is bringing all the figures of her psyche on stage (so to speak) at once to make the layering of self, inner- and intersubjectivity, cut across each other's fault line, each providing necessary connections and links. Real madness is a possibility. But clear demarcations cannot work for Williams, either personally or textually. Mergings make a too full identity crowded with others, while some gaps empty her out from the center. Time and eternity (the threat of extinction) intersect with space and boundaries (inside and out/intrinsic and extrinsic), making her sister's earnest promise of the "fully integrated unmerged individual" (205) an elusive one.

The "comforting spectre of polar bears" rises not only in moments of fear, but in the quiet gap between conferences, "from somewhere deep in [her] psyche," and Williams notes their presence "with satisfaction" (205) as well as fear (207). Since the conferences in question are those of the Modern Language Association and the Association of American Law Schools, the gap is significant: it is the intersections of these disciplines and discourses that enable the genre of legal writing Williams enacts here. Yet, as these bears appear to her, "they hunch and settle and listen from beyond-language" (207). Even after she wakens the eyes remain gleaming at her from the end of the bed. The blur of dream and waking consciousness is terrifying, and Williams is perplexed by her fear of those "fierce dark eyes upon her," believing that the multiple layers of selfhood in voices and visions is "not just intelligent but fashionable, feminist, and even postmodern" (207). Her intellectually sophisticated appreciation of the experience should soften her fear of "their claws and their silence and the accusation in their eyes" (208). But entering the wilderness is not a Disneyland adventure. The bears come to her fully fleshed, with smells of "meat and blood" on their breath, "disguised as insanity itself" (208). The bears function in ways that she understands but cannot control; she can at best "settle in for the vision that their presence will have brought" (208). They work as figures, she says, to help her mark her shifts:

> It is also wise, I know, to maintain some consciousness of where I am when I am other than the voice itself. If the other voice in my head is really me too, then it means that I have shifted positions, ever so slightly, and become a new being, a different one from her over there. It gets confusing sometimes, so I leave markers of where I've been, particularly if it's not just a voice but a place that I want to come back to in time. This season those spots are marked with polar bears. (207–8)

Part of what is powerful here is the "I" as other than "the voice itself," yet enabling, conscious, self-protective. The conventions of postmodern sensibility (as Williams notes) are such that an (even occasionally) integrated sense of self is more remarkable than a fragmented one. Williams claims that integrated "I," mobile, attentive, and able to recognize and assess its own self-differences, and thereby marks a similarity to Jane Flax's notion of a "core" self that is not merely "the effect of thinking or language" but also its cause (*Thinking Fragments* 219). The complexity, Williams notes, gets confusing, and that is stimulus for inventive practice. The "marking" of self's movement, as polar bears do to outline their territory as familiar and possessed, works textually in ways that are recognizable in literary terms.

The bear/self is a recurring presence here, signaled from the beginning in the volume's dedication ("to ... the three bears") and in Williams's sister's early comic transformation as Williams is describing to her how she wants this book to work:

> "I hope that the gaps in my own writing will be self-consciously filled by the reader as an act of forced mirroring of meaning-invention. To this end, I exploit all sorts of literary devices, including parody, parable, and poetry."
>
> "... as in polar bears?" my sister asks eagerly, alert now, ears pricked, nose quivering, hair bristling.
>
> "My, what big teeth you have!" I exclaim, just before the darkness closes over me. (8)

The "mirroring of meaning-invention" (8) that Williams hopes to force the reader into is layered here as she plays outrageously with fantasy, fairy tale, and dramatic modes. But the shifting registers or dimensions of reality of the text and its generic constructions that keep the reader alert, ears pricked, also reflect the polar bear figures in their multiple significations and work as markers for the reader as for Williams herself, letting us know where she has been psychologically, imaginatively, textually. The bears are a comic presence, a way to break up the potential tedium of legal lessons, as when she tells us that "inside, the bears and I panic" (203) in response to students' questions about contract law. They are her aides in the shifting ground of self-conscious subject-object spaces; dream shamans, or "lawyer shamans in a bear mask" (209); a place of "peace" in the clamor of warring voices and vision competing "in the fight to rule [her]" (213). Of the "open space" that is not inhabited by one voice but is a transition zone in which various voices speak, Williams says, "I mark that open space, that shift, with the peace of polar bears. They make strong fashion statements, and they hold for me what I cannot own" (213). Alongside the self-ironizing "fashion statement," Williams is suggesting that the precious property of selfhood is not the whole of self, and that "I" cannot be contained in property imagery. The polar bears "hold" for her what she cannot "own" in a kind of trust. That area is an open space not characterized by black and white, or self and other, but is one that reveals a "different ethic, brought to me," she says, "from a world beyond difference" (213). This ethic crosses all spaces of urban and wilderness life: "Shiny shoes and the need to be seen. Freshly ruffled fur, gleaming with fish oil, sleek with sacrifice" (213). The animal is not only or wholly animal; it is tribal, citified, sensual, dangerous, bestial, and sacred: beyond language, evading every containment.

Access to self that is beyond language, to "I" that in experience is not "voice," fixed not by specific context but by the suggestive passion of the polar bears, Williams contrasts to the mechanical, the cybernetic certainty that promises protection against violation of property. Angered by having his credit cards stolen, Williams's friend is eager for the day that a microchip with personal identification circuitry will be embedded under the skin (211). One's material property and one's "self" will thus be completely conflated by the integration of the machine into the body. The "value" of the person will be indicated in his flesh, just under rather than on the surface of skin, and his bank account number will be made one with his body. Williams envisions the laws that will be written to build "the architecture of embattlement against the heathen and the wilderness" (212) as the "microchip of the well-heeled" (212) becomes another variable in the panic to protect property and the manipulation of the body as a carrier of property value. Self as fortress, secured by advanced machinery and by the abstract machinery of law, is set against the conception of self as participant in "wilderness," inner and outer. For Williams, "wilderness" is in part any dimension of the repressed or the oppressed; thus any stranger, any Other can represent a "wilderness of others" (66).

The source of polar bear power for Williams may be in her godmother's story about a "child who wandered into a world of polar bears, who was prayed over by polar bears, and was in the end eaten. The child's life was not in vain because the polar bears had been made holy by its suffering" (228). The whiteness of polar bears, and the totality of the "polar bear universe" in which the "rest of the living world was fashioned to serve polar bears" (228), make the direct allegory of white domination apparent, and Williams's telling of the effects enlarges the allegory beyond its own borders. The child Patricia wanted true stories: " 'What about roots and that,' I coaxed," but "she would go on telling me about the polar bears until our plates were full of emptiness and I became large in the space that described her emptiness and I gave in to the emptiness of words" (228). The "meaning" of the polar bear story, the parable of the child whose suffering made holy the bears who caused it, requires the listener, the child Patricia and the reader, to shift perspective, to imagine humans "ideally designed [by God] to provide polar bears with meat" (228). As that shift occurs, the possibility of interpretation moves through readings that are shadowed by a long history of the numinous power of sacrifice stories. This story becomes empty in its repeated telling, as the storyteller's own "emptiness" (the "voracity of her amnesia") is inscribed in the repetitions of a single tale. Young Patricia does not get the story of her "roots" and "all that." The food on their plates ("heavy roasts, mashed potatoes, pickles and vanilla pudding") disappears, leaving their plates "full of emptiness": a hunger not satisfied, yet a fullness achieved. The "emptiness of words" seems to carve out a space where the child listening must become large enough to fill up that emptiness, and when Williams says, "I gave in to the emptiness of words" (228), the ambiguity of her assertion is troubling. Words become the "floating signifiers" (7) that allow meanings to rise in context; and words become empty of meaning altogether, and the child surrenders to meaninglessness. The child gets made in the spaces created by the story, and by the storyteller. Words, here, will always be inadequate, and words will always be full of emptiness, thus full of possibility. Both kinds of surrender are implied here. When her godmother, Marjorie, is dying, Williams cares for her:

> My feeding the one who had so often fed me became a complex ritual of mirroring and self-assembly. The physical act of holding the spoon to her lips was not only a rite of nurture and sacrifice, it was the return of a gift.... I bend my head down close to her and listen for mouthed word fragments, sentence crumbs. I bent down to give meaning to her silence, her wandering search for words. (229)

The meaning given to the earlier speaking parallels the meaning given to silence. The two episodes that Williams relates here, the woman caring for the child, the child, now grown, caring for the dying woman are separated by a paragraph narrating Williams's struggles with self-loss:

> There are moments ... when I feel as though a part of me is missing. There are days when I feel so invisible ... when I feel so manipulated that I can't remember my own name.... I have to close my eyes ... and remember myself, draw an internal picture that is smooth and whole; when all else fails, I reach for a mirror and stare myself down until the features reassemble themselves like lost sheep. (228–29)

The self-mirroring that her loving relationship with her godmother provides is a work that she, and her text, must also do for her. When Williams says, "I stare myself down," we feel the will to wholeness, to integration, to connection in battle with the dispersed, the socially violated, manipulated, overdetermined being. The seeing self (the subject or agent) works from within, from the mapped memory of self that is not only experienced but lives in the imaginary as a being that can be figured, drawn as a picture. The uncontrolled materiality of selfhood ("my nose slides around on my face and my eyes drip down to my chin" [228]) requires the discipline, the objectness, the objectivity made possible by the seer-seen connection. The mirror figure, both in one's own hands and as an aspect of loving intersubjectivity, is one of power, and this is the power of "rights." Resisting manipulation, remembering one's own name, are dimensions of power; and "rights," says Williams, "contain images of power, and manipulating those images, either visually or linguistically, is central in the making and maintenance of rights" (234). Making images for herself of herself works actively to resist the alternate, the racist and misogynist visions that work against the entrenching of rights. The "more dizzyingly diverse the images that are propagated" she says, "the more empowered we will be as a society" (234). The individual face in the mirror and the diverse images of her society reflect each other here. The polar bear stories and the deathbed of her godmother form a bridge across the dissolution of selfhood, the losses of face and name. Williams recreates a mirror in the textual processes that layer, link, and blur the images and discourses, a mirror not only of Williams' face for her own perusal and self-assembly, but also to refract the wild diversity of her intimate and disparate commitments.

Polar bears, primary denizens of the metaphorical wilderness, are not just models of the interior or psychological aspects of the denied, or signifiers of hope for engagement with silenced parts of the self. Polar bears also exist, and their real presence in the world intercedes with Williams's use of them to mark boundaries of selfhood and community.

"polar bear musings"

More polar bear stories must be told here. In one Williams juxtaposes a lyrical, almost mystical passage with a blunt news report:

> In reality, it was a lovely polar-bear afternoon. The gentle force of the earth. A wide wilderness of islands. A conspiracy of polar bears lost in timeless forgetting. A gentleness of polar bears, a fruitfulness of polar bears, a silent black-eyed interest of polar bears, a bristled expectancy of polar bears. With the wisdom of innocence, a child threw stones at the polar bears. Hungry in nests, they rose, inquisitive, dark-souled, patient with foreboding, fearful in tremendous awakening. The instinctual ferocity of the hunter reflected upon the hunted. Then, proud teeth and warrior claws took innocence for wilderness and raging insubstantiality for tender rabbit breath.
>
> In the newspapers the next day, it was reported that two polar bears in the Brooklyn Zoo mauled to death an eleven-year-old boy who had entered their cage to swim in the moat. The police were called and the bears were killed. (234)

The beauty of the first paragraph sits uneasily with the baldness of the next. For the reader who has tracked polar bears through their activity in Williams's emotional life, seeing them as various kinds of metaphors and signifiers, as well as narrative structures and psychological figures, the first passage is a floating, lulling affair: a "lovely polar-bear afternoon" in which a "conspiracy," a "gentleness," a "fruitfulness" of polar bears makes the opening phrase "In reality" a signal that the reality Williams refers to is the one she lives in, in which polar bear presences are nurturant. The rhythm of this paragraph is such that when the child, in the "wisdom of innocence" throws stones, the mood stays in the mythic and we do not assume a factual element; but the passage shifts in quiet ways, to the unpredictable, the silent quality of the beasts: "inquisitive, dark-souled, patient." The bears, "fearful in tremendous awakening," reflect earlier reference to the somnambulistic polar bears in the British Zoo whose trancelike psychosis was to be corrected by giving them unbreakable toys (202). The text seems to shiver here as the phrase "In reality" moves the polar bears from containment in Patricia Williams's mind and places her in their universe, the one carved out by her godmother's story. The actual, factual news report of the death of the "eleven-year-old boy" and the killing of the "two polar bears in the Brooklyn Zoo" makes the "in reality" space one that overlaps with the lyrical, but escapes some of its edges. With the descent into fact, Williams shifts registers once more and rehearses the public debates, the contradictory responses to the bears and to the child, also an inhabitant of a wilderness, "born into the urban jungle of a black welfare mother and a Hispanic alcoholic father" (234). The rhetoric of these debates, Williams notes, firmly establishes that "both were innocent, naturally territorial, unfairly imprisoned, and guilty" (234). The conflation here of the zoo creatures and the young boy in the contradictions of public narrative reinforces Williams's readings of "wilderness" or othering.

The divergence of public perspectives, and the creation of meaning that accrues, becomes evidence in her own narrative of legal rights debates. Making herself into the third person, Williams frames the event this way, inserting herself into the drama as a conference speaker: "the keynote speaker unpacked the whole incident as a veritable laboratory of emergent rights discourse. Just seeing that these complex levels of meaning exist, she exulted, should advance the discourse significantly" (235). Laying the "emergent rights discourse" alongside her autographical discourse of polar bear musings, Williams parallels the interior flow of poetic language with social critique, and concludes the episode with the information that at the boy's funeral the priest announced that the boy's death had saved him from a life of crime: "Juan's Hispanic-welfare-black-widow-of-an-alcoholic mother decided then and there to sue" (235). The rhetorical gestures here, the hyphens, the dramatic decision, the litigation so instantly to hand, and the open-ended question, sue whom?, leave the text with the reductive and reassuring fact: Mrs. Perez has rights.

"a propagation of me's ... strong single-hearted"

Williams's "polar-bear musings," in which black and white, speech and silence, wilderness and safety are not easily separated from one another, and no plain valuation stands, are all necessary, and all are part of "a complexity of messages implied in our being" (236). Messages require reading, interpretation. The texts of self-reading and self-writing are implicated in the contradictions of color and colorlessness. She shows us the hope, peace, trust, and strength of "pastel polar-bear moments" like those of the shaman in the bear-mask of her dream, whose dance and whose beneficent presence leaves Williams awakening, conscious of "a propagation of me's," "strong, single-hearted" (201).

Her conclusion presents her ambiguously "manumitted back into silence," freed for the moment by her outraged cry against a lumpish group of white adolescent boys who have jostled her off the sidewalk: "See me! And deflect Goddammit!" (235). Her defiant, proud and loud claim, "I have my rights!" (235), allows her to give herself over to beyond-language, where she allows bear spirits to "watch over" her. Musing her way into the uncertain ease, she finds "a clean white wind," in a "white wilderness of icy meateaters heavy with remembrance ... shaggy with the effort of hunting for silence" (236). In this polar bear universe, Williams finds "cool moments of white-fur invisibility. Solid, black-gummed, intent, observant. Hungry and patient, impassive and exquisitely timed. The brilliant bursts of exclusive territoriality" (236). Whiteness, here, is almost liberated from its racialized designation, in the "clean white wind," and resituated in racial identity in the icy landscape and white-fur camouflage. All elements of Williams's selfhood and self-writing take up space in this dreamy, tough passage. The black and white, the speaking presence, and the vitality and freedom of silence exist alongside the solitary and the communal, the liberty of invisibility and the power of self-possession. Messages are implied in "our" being: a generous sharing of vision, of resistance, of a beyond-language possibility. Williams's autography, entering the wilderness of antiracist self-construction, makes writing from her particular context a celebration without sentimentality, an exploration of parts without sacrificing center, an exposure of vulnerability without the inscription of victimhood, an affirmation of the reader's position without surrendering to the space of the totally read. *The Alchemy of Race and Rights* makes the alchemy of autography a catalyst in resistant, emancipatory discourse.

CHAPTER FIVE

Selves: Intersecting

"Self" (that old-fashioned word I refuse to surrender) in the writing at the heart of this study has been consistently problematized, unstable, and fluid—and present. My discussion has resisted hypostasis into a single semiotics or register, and "I"-ness has appeared here as subjectivity, agency, interpellated identities, or simply selfhood. The strong presence of the "I" in feminist discourse continually reasserts the belief that the personal is political—one of the basic principles of feminist consciousness. Moreover, it suggests how forcefully the self is an inescapable issue in feminist ideology. Contrary to the fear of some feminist thinkers that the political becomes merely personal in concerns about selfhood, as in Sheila Rowbotham's feeling that the "slogan" "tends to imply that all individual problems can find a short term political solution" (*Beyond the Fragments* 31), the familiar phrasing continues to undergo changes in interpretation and in its power to inspire transformation. In Teresa de Lauretis's words, self-consciousness as feminist process is

> a recasting of the notion that the personal is the political which does not simply equate and collapse the two ... but maintains the tension between

them precisely through the understanding of identity as multiple and even self-contradictory. ("Feminist Studies" 9)

As women's senses of self in the world are modified in the process of an evolving feminist consciousness, the context too is understood differently. Self, as a political issue, is the basis from which women have resisted the definitions and designations of various male authorities (religious, psychoanalytic, literary, or political — right or left). And it is the basis from which feminists of color have resisted the assumptions of white feminists who have inappropriately generalized from their own experience to that of all women.[1]

Feminist self-writing invites a consideration of relations of difference as self and community embody (each and both) difference from and difference within. The recognition, acknowledgment, acceptance, and, most importantly, the definition of "difference" are ideological and ethical issues for feminists of every context. Gloria Anzaldúa notes that "difference" is likely to be "defined differently by whitefeminists and feminists-of-color" (*Making Face* xxi). Trinh T. Minh-ha says that "difference should be defined neither by the dominant sex nor by the dominant culture" ("Difference" 5). June Jordan, shifting away from definition of identity or difference as a predetermined category, argues that "given identity, whether it's gender or race ... [*sic*] is just too simple" ("Craft that Politics Requires" 34). Jordan emphasizes "what this person has *chosen,* or what this person would like to choose, for himself, herself, or for the world" (34). Insisting on the need for explicit antiracist work, rather than assuming antiracism as a given of feminist thought, for example, is one aspect of feminist practice that may allow the ideas of difference to be demystified, deessentialized, and the material (i.e., racist, homophobic) effects of power-over to be challenged. Shirley Neuman takes up the problem of "difference" as a category, and argues for a "poetics of differences" that would allow the writing of a self, "not only constructed by differences but capable of choosing, inscribing, and making a difference" ("Autobiography: From a Different Poetics" 224–25). Difference, then, like sameness, that is, a reified category based on a principle of an essential binary, may distract from coalition building. Moreover, the valorizing of ideas of "difference" that have evolved

in a racist context is deeply vulnerable to a reiteration of white supremacy: that is, "difference" will be marked as the terrain of people
of color, while "sameness" will blank out the limits of whiteness
(Frankenberg, *White Women, Race Matters* 197). At home as well as
in the geopolitics of transnational feminism, many women are rejecting the (American?) fantasy of "unitary feminism in favor of solidarity and coalitions that are not based on mystified notions of
similarity and difference" (Kaplan "Politics" of Location" 148). The
mutually transformative relations (the edges that blur) between the
person, her cultural and racial context, her feminist communities,
and the dominant culture are continuously shifting. As the interior
and exterior (self/culture/community) groupings gain and lose specific distinctions, the dividing lines within the self and within one's
various "worlds" blur, reform, shift, and regroup. The extent to which
the feminist community exists *as* writing is based in part on the writing of these complexities of feminist subjectivity. This writing (of)
multiple selves, tracing the various relations of power, and develop-
ing resistances to the dominant internalized and external discourses,
in large part constitutes a feminist community.

Norma Alarcón's view that "to privilege the subject, even if multi-
ple-voiced, is not enough" ("Theoretical Subject(s)" 366) underlies the
argument that material, social, historical reality requires more of feminist practice and theory than autographics can supply. Yet, the idea
of "rights" that Patricia Williams discusses in American terms brings
the speaking voices of women saying "I" to the fore and grounds in-
dividual/community ideas of women as persons with rights interna-
tionally. The United Nations World Conference on Human Rights
held in June 1993 in Vienna, the largest gathering ever on that issue,
was confronted by an international group of thousands of women
who were there to ensure that women's rights were incorporated
into the United Nations Declaration of Human Rights. The coalition
of women from around the world who brought their stories to the
conference was an extraordinary example of global "sisterhood."[2] The
Vienna Tribunal consisted of individual women standing before a
panel of human rights specialists narrating their experiences. The personal voice speaking "I" as witness to her own suffering and the United

Nations's subsequent inclusion of women's rights in its Declaration of Human Rights (October 1993) testify to the power of the individual voice in the context of an international feminist coalition. The process that brought thirty-three women from twenty-seven countries together to testify before thousands of other women involved two full years of organizing. The dynamics of selecting those testimonies, shaping them, and working through the women's personal, cultural, locational, and ideological differences to allow the power of their narratives to come through touches this study of autography: the embodied self, articulated in the context of a feminist community, is essential to that community, and changes (a little at a time) the world. This instance of transnational feminist solidarity seems to be cutting through the hegemonic impulses of dominant-group (including North American feminist) discourses, and demonstrating what is possible.[3]

Unlike the concerns of mainstream criticism, which must remind itself of the "ideological subtext which any critical theory reflects and embodies, and the relation which this subtext bears to the production of meaning" (Gates, "*Race,*" *Writing, and Difference* 15), the ideologies of feminist discourse, including (and especially) feminist autography, are not embedded in subtexts but are the texts themselves. I do not mean to suggest that feminist writing has no "unconscious," that feminist writers of the self have certain privileged powers of language that allow them to escape the internal contradictions that befall other writers, but rather that feminist autographers invite their own differences to work as correction.

Autography is as much a reading practice as it is a mode of writing. Because it focuses on the textual configurations of subjectivity rather than on the narratives of life history, it can cross through conventional genres and provide a name for those modes of expression that refuse to accommodate familiar forms. Had I chosen other texts, other writers, the "conclusions" would not have been different, because no conclusions can be drawn—except those that affirm the processes that the texts and writers enact. Giving voice to that which has been silenced is consistent in the ethics and actions of contemporary feminists. The individual writer inscribes her self, in one voice or many. But bringing to speech parts of one's self that one has had reason to keep silent is frightening, painful, and even dangerous. An analogous process takes place in the feminist community as voices demand the right to be heard, and to be heard on the same basis or principle on which the women's movement is grounded: the worth of individual or personal selfhood. When that self no longer is seen either as a monad, an isolated and alienated being, hearing only its own echoes, shoring its fragments only against its own ruin, or as an interpellated construct, existing only as another discourse, then writing the self can be recognized as a social and political act. Most feminists in the United States have chosen not to abandon the principle of personal identity, but rather to discover in it, through various processes, subjectivities as complex as the communities that make up its discourse. Only an ideology of extraordinary flexibility can inform and embody the varied shades of feminist selfhood as it is articulated within and by feminist autography. And only an ideology that embraces transformation as its heart can fulfill this possibility.

Audre Lorde's writing of her specifically female cancer as a "Black lesbian feminist experience" makes in the writing a community of women of all colors and sexual orientations who are subject to breast cancer. That she could write it, however, is made possible by her particular strengths, *and* by the living community of women around her. Kate Millett's multiple and deeply personal writing of self speaks of the communal consciousness of a feminist identification with other women. Like Adrienne Rich's, Kate Millett's allegiance with women is neither safe nor easy. It requires a recognition of one's self in the mad woman, the victim, the vicious one, not only because of one's own hidden madness or weakness, but because of certain shared conditions in the material and the discursive worlds. In Rich, history is personal and communal, and the self, in its dialectical engagement with reality, is the precise embodiment of history. Patricia Williams extends autographics into a discourse whose aim is to suppress the particularity of lived experience. Williams's claim to possess self and to inhabit a process of subjectivity acknowledges objective history and opens possibilities of thought and feeling about identity. Each writer whom this study has discussed makes her "self" the ground of her writing and the scene of her choices, and that writing becomes the ground of her (and our) community. The process is recursive: the selves written are transformed in the writing as the communities they change change them. Feminism, subjectivity, and autography together give us the space to ask ourselves, with Audre Lorde, "What are the words you do not yet have? What do you need to say?" (*Sister/ Outsider* 41).

~

Notes

1. Autography/Transformation/Asymmetry

1. I refer here to "numbers" of speakers: women of every community or context have, I believe, always been speaking, but only when some critical mass (or volume) is achieved does that "speaking" seem to be heard. And it can be said to be "heard" when its effects make their way into a mainstream of institutional, public life (the media, the education system, the courts).

2. For other uses of this word see Michael Ryan, "Self-Evidence" 6; Jane Gallop, "*Writing and Sexual Difference:* The Difference Within" 284; Domna C. Stanton, ed., *The Female Autograph*; and Elizabeth Meese, *(Sem)Erotics* 79.

3. Here, referring to the United States.

4. For my purposes, "a feminist" is she who claims the name—though obviously not all practices of feminists can be called feminist practices. As for "feminism," Gayatri Spivak's description of "the best of French feminism" continues to have the virtues of clarity, spaciousness, and inclusiveness: "*against* sexism, where women unite as a biologically oppressed caste; and *for* feminism where human beings train to prepare for a transformation of consciousness" ("French Feminism in an International Frame," in *In Other Worlds* 145).

5. Riley's sensitivity to naming is the basis of her study, and she is committed to a feminism that includes "female persons" and rejects a postfeminist indifference to "the stubborn harshness of lived gender" ("*Am I That Name?*" 3); her anxiety, however, about claiming the power of naming seems to lie at the heart of her insistence that women can exist only within quotation marks (as "women").

6. Readers should note Elspeth Probyn's discussion of distinctions between strategy and tactic. See *Sexing the Self,* esp. 86–107.

7. "Obsessive" is my word, not hers. Jardine uses "paranoiac," 117.

8. Jardine casts the designation of "mother tongue" into doubt: she says, slyly, "It would seem, in fact, to be the mother who has the language, the maternal tongue, necessary for all these writers in modernity; or *at least* that language which according to Lacan escapes the self, the Cartesian ego—the *la langue* of literature" (116, my emphasis). She cites the case of Louis Wolfson, whose abhorrence of his mother's presence and voice caused him to construct a labrynthian secret language involving "cutting up his maternal tongue in a mysterious and sophisticated way" (116). What interests Jardine is the French theorists' view of Wolfson as "exemplary of modernity's rejection of the Cartesian subject, the sign, and representation."

9. Feminism and psychoanalysis enjoy a fiercely complex relationship, with feminists taking and making stands on every aspect of the Freudian, Lacanian, and object-relations debates. Readers with a particular interest should note especially *Between Feminism and Psychoanalysis*, edited by Teresa Brennan, and *Feminism and Psychoanalytic Theory*, by Nancy J. Chodorow, esp. 163–98.

10. Indeed, some men are said to write "in the feminine." Whereas a woman writer who seemed to be clear or energetic or forceful was often said to write "like a man"— transcending her femaleness—men who write "in the feminine" (James Joyce, for example) lose nothing of their maleness or their status as respected writers and gain from being said to have special insight into "the female."

11. Julia Kristeva distinguishes between the "semiotic" and "symbolic" stages of infant development. A reductive outline of her theory suggests that in the semiotic stage the "preoedipal" child, still in mother's realm, makes sounds undifferentiated as signifiers. The "symbolic" stage occurs when the child splits from mother and enters language, in which submission to "meaning, sign, and the signified object" manifest the oedipal identification with the father and his laws. See *Desire in Language*, 133–34. The "semiotic" stage (sometimes referred to as the "[m]Other tongue") later returns as "poetic" discourse—rhythm, disruption of grammar, and so on. The "Other" is necessarily a "feminine" presence, and the "subject" that emerges through the endless discourse that constitutes life (or the psychic life at least) must necessarily be male—otherwise, whence "Otherness?" See Luce Irigaray, "Any Theory of the 'Subject' Has Always Been Appropriated by the 'Masculine,'"in *Speculum of the Other Woman*, 133–46.

12. See Gayatri Spivak's discussion of "the suppression of the clitoris . . . as the suppression of the woman-in-excess" in "French Feminism in an International Frame," in *In Other Worlds*, 152.

13. See especially Jacques Derrida, "Structure, Sign and Play in the Discourse of the Human Sciences," in *Writing and Difference*, 278–80.

14. This generalization about the woman writer could (and should) be made also about the male writer. Both are privileged in the same way. Conversely, both male and female writers argue that "writing transcends sexual identity" (Miller, "Changing" 107). This is a disagreement that we cannot solve. The resolution depends on a shared understanding, that is to say, ideology.

15. Derrida himself seems to authorize some forms of the authorial subject when he asserts, "The 'subject' of writing does not exist if we mean by that some sovereign solitude of the author" ("Freud and the Scene of Writing," in *Writing and Difference* 226).

16. Naomi Schor's "This Essentialism Which Is Not One: Coming to Grips with Irigaray" looks especially at Irigaray's discussion of "feminine fluidity," and asserts that Irigaray's "best defense against essentialism is the defiant plurality of the feminine" (n. 6, 56). Plurality, in metaphor at least, can lead to a universalizing impulse as we observe in the unfortunate appropriations of racial and sexual experience in Cixous: "we the re-

pressed of our culture ... we are black and we are beautiful" ("Laugh of the Medusa" 248), and "we are all Lesbians" (252).

17. A succinct treatment of *écriture feminine* appears in the introduction to the issue of *Cultural Critique* on "The Construction of Gender and Modes of Social Division I," edited by Donna Przyblowicz, Nancy Hartsock, and Pamela McCallum.

18. Contrast this with Judith's Butler's suggestion that "we may seek recourse to matter in order to ground or to verify a set of injuries or violations only to find that *matter itself is founded through a set of violations*" (Bodies That Matter 29).

19. Jardine is discussing Lacan's assertion that "there is always something about and in her which escapes discourse," taken from *Seminaire II* 34. Quoted in *Gynesis*, 165.

20. Tania Modleski notes that Butler's "highly abstract Foucauldian meditation" never deals with the issue of gender intersection with race, class, or regional specificities, though Butler criticizes "essentialist" feminists (those who position themselves as women) for ignoring those very "modalities" (*Feminism Without Women* 18).

21. Butler's *Bodies That Matter* (1993) addresses itself to some of these criticisms, and foregrounds the problems of materiality, asking a familiar question: "Can language simply refer to materiality, or is language also the very condition under which materiality may be said to appear?" (31).

22. Butler (25) is quoting from *On the Genealogy of Morals*, trans. Walter Kaufman (New York: Vintage, 1969) 45.

23. See Shirley Neuman's discussion "Autobiography, Bodies, Manhood."

24. Contrast this phrasing with Elspeth Probyn's provocative reading of Foucault's "care of the self": "The self is a line of analysis that articulates the epistemological and the ontological" (*Sexing* 128).

25. To think of Audre Lorde as "disfigured" by her mastectomy may be inevitable, but if this text works as I believe it does, she can been seen in a new and positive configuration of selfhood.

26. The Lesbian and Literature Panel of the Modern Language Association, December 28, 1977.

27. Jerome Brooks, "In the Name of the Father: The Poetry of Audre Lorde." Brooks says of this "brave little book" that the subtitle of the second chapter, "A Black Lesbian Feminist Experience," "is valid only to identify the author; beyond one discreet episode some twenty-five years earlier that took place in Mexico, it does not characterize what is in the text" (275). The title of his essay makes further comment unnecessary.

28. Black and white, lesbian, bisexual, and straight, 20, 28, 29, 30, 37, 39.

2. Adrienne Rich: A Poetics of Subjectivity

1. See "Integrity" — "*Nothing but myself?... My selves*" (Fact 274).

2. That is, the U.S. variety of American — a necessary distinction, one that she is increasingly careful to make, and one that other North Americans (Mexicans and Canadians) can appreciate.

3. I am referring to a general impression formed, mostly, by the personal writing in *Of Woman Born*, esp. 1–15, 190–93, 257–59; and various passages in the essays in *On Lies, Secrets, and Silence*.

4. See the Combahee River Collective, *This Bridge Called My Back*, 212.

5. Caren Kaplan's discussion of "the politics of location" argues that Rich suppresses the influence of U.S. women of color on her thinking. I do not find Kaplan's critique persuasive, and I suggest readers go back to the original essays for insight into how scrupulously Rich attends to the question "Who is *we*?" (*Blood* 231). See Kaplan, "Politics of Location," esp. 139–41.

6. Ruth Frankenberg's powerful analysis of "the social construction of whiteness" argues that antiracism requires "whiteness" to be "delimited and 'localized'" (*White Women, Race Matters* 231). Rich has been among the earliest of antiracist white women to begin exploring publicly the ways in which whiteness has shaped her experience.

7. This is the wrong word—some parts of this landscape may be present already, laid out, while others, surely, are established in the acts of writing this identity.

8. Since Jewish heritage is passed through the maternal line, the fact that Rich's father, not her mother, was Jewish makes her struggle to find/create her Jewishness very complex. Moreover, her father disguised the fact that he was a Jew.

9. Adrienne Rich, "One Kind of Terror: A Love Poem," in *Your Native Land, Your Life,* 50–55.

10. *Sources* first appeared through Woodside, California: Heyeck Press, 1983. I use the more accessible "Sources" in *Your Native Land, Your Life: Poems,* 3–27.

11. See also "Split at the Root: An Essay on Jewish Identity," in *Blood.*

12. We may wish to link this to the "perfection of order" that Rich felt was so limiting in her early poetry.

13. That the limitations of "the correct line" distress Rich is apparent in "North American Time," in which she says, "When my dreams showed signs / of becoming / politically correct / ... then I began to wonder" (*Your Native Land, Your Life* 33). Readers should recall that Rich was using the expression "politically correct" when it still belonged to the left, when it still signaled part of our own self-correction and was not a reactionary term.

14. Rich, "Contradictions: Tracking Poems," in *Your Native Land, Your Life,* 83–111. References to these twenty-nine poems will be by number and page and will appear in the text.

15. Audre Lorde's conflict with those who wished to gag her pain with the pretense of a false breast demonstrates Rich's point.

16. Readers of the first poem will certainly think of Eliot's *The Waste Land*: Rich reminds us that "April is the cruelest month" in her warning that "the worst moment of winter can come in April" ("Contradictions" 1), and when she says, "our bodies / plod on without conviction" (1) we may recall "I had not thought death had undone so many." Her presence and personal engagement with the wasteland of cold and pain in which Adrienne Rich finds herself, however, make this poem diverge profoundly from Eliot's. See T. S. Eliot, *The Waste Land* in *The Complete Poems and Plays: 1909–1950,* 37–55.

17. See "One Art," Elizabeth Bishop, *The Collected Poems, 1927–1979,* 178.

3. Kate Millett's *The Basement*: Testimony of the Unspeakable

1. For a frustrated reader's view see Joyce Carol Oates's review of *The Basement* in the *New York Times Book Review* (September 9, 1979), 14.

2. The disease of hysterics. See Hélène Cixous and Catherine Clément, *The Newly Born Woman,* 34.

3. One point of similarity may be the monotony. Roland Barthes says, "Sade is *monotonous*," *Sade/Fourier/Loyola,* 36; the word Millett makes Sylvia repeat endlessly as she nears death is "monotony" (277). We might wonder at the monotony of Millett's repetitions as well.

4. Peggy Phelan's discussion of the "double action" that is the "lure of the image repertoire" explains some of the poignancy of Millett's tone: "The double action confirms the distinction between the gaze and the eye: the eye, ever hungry, ever restless, temporarily submits to the law of the gaze, the ocular perspective which frames the image, sees what is shown and discovers it to be 'lacking'" (*Unmarked* 34).

5. The following report appeared in the University of Toronto student newspaper: "Several campus groups are up in arms over a September 8 incident involving some male engineers and a female inflatable doll.//The doll episode occurred during the U of T's Engineering Society's 1987 orientation. Several engineering students used beer bottles to simulate various sex acts in what several witnesses called a gang rape.... Engineering Society Vice President (Activities) Keren Morehead said, 'It's not supposed to be a gang rape.... It's supposed to be fun.'" In *The Varsity: The Undergraduate Newspaper* (October 1, 1987).

6. Readers may wish to compare this with the use of tubs in the torture Elaine Scarry describes in *The Body in Pain,* 43–44.

7. Millett takes the phrasings from Gertrude's testimony, in which she pleaded innocent, blaming all the violence on the youngsters admitting only that she once "tried" to whip the girl (119, n. 15; 131, n. 26).

8. Jacobo Timerman, *Prisoner without a Name,* esp. 61, 132. This book, read parallel with *The Basement,* is deeply informative. The ideological and experiential relationship between Timerman's suffering in prison and Sylvia Likens's in the house on New York Street is instructive for the kinds of civil rights and privileges Timerman enjoyed that Sylvia had no access to. Nevertheless, the hatred of his Jewishness and the hatred of Sylvia's femaleness are close. We cannot assume these are merely the ideological "readings" of Millett and Timerman. The torture and the words were both real.

9. Scarry discusses at length the "remaking of the human body into an artifact" in *The Body in Pain.* See esp. 38–40, 243–45, 161–69.

4. Patricia Williams's *Alchemy:* "my most precious property, I"

1. This term is from Judith Fetterly's *The Resisting Reader.*

2. Nancy K. Miller suggests that reciting the "litany of RaceClassGender" be changed to "doing something" in *Getting Personal,* xiii.

3. The vision of an unremitting exercise of "pure will," or its binary will-lessness, seems to overlap uncomfortably with subjectivity theory here as the polarities of "agency" and "interpellation" take up the rhetorical space vacated by those nineteenth-century discourses of will.

4. Comparison with the inscription on Sylvia Likens's body ("I am a prostitute and proud of it") suggests that the inscription of crime on this young girl's body was her race, not her sex; but she was punished for both with rape and torture.

5. She quotes an editor (or a composite of editors) who chides her for her use of the word "schizophrenia" and who helpfully explains, "'schizophrenia is a serious disability afflicting millions'" (214). The overwriting that this editing from the outside represents conveys Williams's suffocation.

5. Selves: Intersecting

1. In addition to explorations of "whiteness" undertaken by Adrienne Rich, Marilyn Frye, Minnie Bruce Pratt, and Judy Grahn familiar to feminist readers, Ruth Frankenberg's *White Women, Race Matters* offers profound insight into how white women see themselves racially.

2. See *The Vienna Tribunal,* a documentary directed by Gerry Rogers, coproduced by Augusta Productions and the National Film Board, St. John's, Newfoundland, Canada.

3. I take Caren Kaplan's point that North American women cannot be homogenized into a single group or positionality. Nevertheless, national character does leave its mark, as the narratives of African American women in African nations attest, or as U.S. feminists (of color and white) in Canada demonstrate. See Kaplan's "The Politics of Location as Transnational Feminist Critical Practice," esp. 138–41.

Bibliography

Abel, Elizabeth, ed. *Writing and Sexual Difference.* Chicago: University of Chicago Press, 1982.

Alarcón, Norma. "The Theoretical Subject(s) of *This Bridge Called My Back* and Anglo-American Feminism." In Anzaldúa, ed., *Making Face.* 356–69.

Althusser, Louis. *Essays on Ideology.* London: Verso, 1984.

Altieri, Charles. *Self and Sensibility in Contemporary American Poetry.* Cambridge: Cambridge University Press, 1984.

Anzaldúa, Gloria. "*En Rapport,* In Opposition: *Cobrando Cuentas A Las Nuestras.*" *Sinister Wisdom* 33 (1987): 11–17.

——, ed. *Making Face, Making Soul. Haciendo Caras: Creative and Critical Perspectives by Women of Color.* San Francisco: Aunt Lute, 1990.

Bal, Mieke. *Narratology: Introduction to the Theory of Narrative.* Trans. Christine van Boheemen. Toronto: University of Toronto Press, 1985.

Barthes, Roland. *The Pleasure of the Text.* Trans. Richard Miller. New York: Hill and Wang, 1975.

——. *Roland Barthes by Roland Barthes.* New York: Hill and Wang, 1977.

——. *The Rustle of Language.* Trans. Richard Howard. New York: Hill and Wang, 1986.

——. *Sade/Fourier/Loyola.* Trans. Richard Miller. New York: Hill and Wang, 1976.

Baudrillard, Jean. *Simulations.* Trans. Paul Foss, Paul Patton, and Philip Beitchman. New York: Semiotext(e), 1983.

Bellour, Raymond. "Interview with Roland Barthes." Trans. Christine Saxton. *Discourse* 2 (1980): 3–16.

Belsey, Catherine. "Constructing the subject: deconstructing the text." In *Feminist Criticism and Social Change: Sex, Class and Race in Literature and Culture.* Ed. Judith Newton and Deborah Rosenfelt. New York and London: Methuen, 1985. 45–64.

————. *Critical Practice.* London and New York: Methuen, 1980.

————. "The Romantic Construction of the Unconscious." In *Literature, Politics and Theory: Papers from the Essex Conference, 1976–1984.* Ed. Francis Barker et al. London and New York: Methuen, 1986. 57–76.

Benstock, Shari, ed. *Feminist Issues in Literary Scholarship.* Bloomington: Indiana University Press, 1987.

————, ed. *The Private Self: Theory and Practice of Women's Autobiographical Writings.* Chapel Hill and London: University of North Carolina Press, 1988.

Bishop, Elizabeth. "One Art." In *The Complete Poems, 1927–1979.* New York: Farrar, Straus and Giroux, 1983. 178.

Bordo, Susan. " 'Material Girl': The Effacements of Postmodern Culture." In *The Female Body: Figures, Styles, Speculations.* Ed. Laurence Goldstein. Ann Arbor: University of Michigan Press, 1991. 106–30.

Brant, Beth, ed. *Sinister Wisdom: A Gathering of Spirit: North American Indian Women's Issue.* Iowa City: Iowa City Women's Press, 1983.

Brennan, Teresa, ed. *Between Feminism and Psychoanalysis.* London and New York: Routledge, 1989.

Brooks, Jerome. "In the Name of the Father: The Poetry of Audre Lorde." In *Black Women Writers (1950–1980): A Critical Evaluation.* Ed. Mari Evans. New York: Anchor, 1984. 269–76.

Brossard, Nicole. *These Our Mothers or: The Disintegrating Chapter.* Trans. Barbara Godard. Toronto: Coach House, 1983.

Butler, Christopher. *Interpretation, Deconstruction, and Ideology.* Oxford: Clarendon Press, 1984.

Butler, Judith. *Gender Trouble: Feminism and the Subversion of Identity.* New York and London: Routledge, 1990.

————. *Bodies That Matter: On the Discursive Limits of "Sex."* New York and London: Routledge, 1993.

Byers, Thomas B. "Adrienne Rich: Vision as Rewriting." In *World, Self, and Poem: Essays on Contemporary Poetry from the "Jubilation of Poets."* Ed. Leonard M. Trawick. Kent, Ohio, and London, England: Kent State University Press, 1990. 144–52.

Cascardi, Anthony J. *The Subject of Modernity.* Cambridge: Cambridge University Press, 1992.

Caws, Mary Ann. "Ladies Shot and Painted: Female Embodiment in Surrealist Art." In Suleiman, ed., *Female Body.* 262–87.

Chodorow, Nancy J. *Feminism and Psychoanalytic Theory.* New Haven and London: Yale University Press, 1989.

Christian, Barbara. "Connections and Distinctions." Review of *Specifying: Black Women Writing the American Experience* by Susan Willis. *Women's Review of Books* July–August (1987): 25–26.

Chrystos. "I Am Not Your Princess." *Sinister Wisdom* 33 (1987): 18–19.

Cixous, Hélène. "The Laugh of the Medusa." In *New French Feminisms: An Anthology.* Trans. Keith Cohen and Paula Cohen. Ed. Elaine Marks and Isabelle de Courtivron. New York: Schocken, 1980. 245–64.

————, and Catherine Clément. *The Newly Born Woman.* Trans. Betsy Wing. Minneapolis: University of Minnesota Press, 1986.

Cliff, Michelle. *Claiming an Identity They Taught Me to Despise.* Watertown, Mass.: Persephone Press, 1980.

Collins, Patricia Hill. *Black Feminist Thought: Knowledge, Consciousness and the Politics of Empowerment.* London: HarperCollins Academic, 1990.

Combahee River Collective. "A Black Feminist Statement." In Moraga and Anzaldúa, eds., *This Bridge*. 210–18.

Cooper, Jane Roberta, ed. *Reading Adrienne Rich: Reviews and Re-Visions, 1951–1981*. Ann Arbor: University of Michigan Press, 1984.

Culler, Jonathan. *On Deconstruction: Theory and Criticsm after Structuralism*. Ithaca, N. Y.: Cornell University Press, 1982.

———. *The Pursuit of Signs: Semiotics, Literature, Deconstruction*. Ithaca, N.Y.: Cornell University Press, 1981.

Culpepper, Emily Erwin. "Simone de Beauvoir and the Revolt of the Symbols." *Trivia: A Journal of Ideas* 6 (1985): 6–32.

Daly, Mary. *Beyond God the Father: Toward a Philosophy of Women's Liberation*. Boston: Beacon, 1973.

———. *Gyn/Ecology: The Metaethics of Radical Feminism*. Boston: Beacon, 1983.

———. *Pure Lust: Elemental Feminist Philosophy*. Boston: Beacon, 1984.

de Lauretis, Teresa. *Alice Doesn't: Feminism, Semiotics, Cinema*. Bloomington: Indiana University Press, 1984.

———. "The Essence of the Triangle or Taking the Risk of Essentialism Seriously: Feminist Theory in Italy, the U.S. and Britain." *differences* 1.2 (Summer 1989): 3–37.

———. "Feminist Studies/Critical Studies: Issues, Terms, and Contexts." In *Feminist Studies/Critical Studies*. Ed. Teresa de Lauretis. Bloomington: Indiana University Press, 1986. 1–20.

———. *Technologies of Gender*. Bloomington: Indiana University Press, 1987.

de Man, Paul. "Autobiography as De-facement." *Modern Language Notes* 94 (1979): 919–30.

Derrida, Jacques. *The Ear of the Other*. New York: Schocken, 1985.

———. *Writing and Difference*. Trans. Alan Bass. London: Routledge and Kegan Paul, 1978.

Diaz-Diocaretz, Myriam. "Black North-American Women Poets in the Semiotics of Culture." In *Women, Feminist Identity, and Society in the 1980's*. Ed. Myriam Diaz-Diocaretz and Iris Zavala. Amsterdam/Philadelphia: John Benjamins Publishing, 1985. 37–60.

———. *The Transforming Power of Language: The Poetry of Adrienne Rich*. Utrecht: HES Publishers, 1984.

———. *Translating Poetic Discourse: Questions of Feminist Strategies in Adrienne Rich*. Amsterdam/Philadelphia: John Benjamins Publishing, 1985.

Donovan, Josephine. "Toward a Women's Poetics." In Benstock, ed., *Feminist Issues*. 98–109.

Du Bois, W. E. B. *The Souls of Black Folk: Essays and Sketches*. 1903. New York: Fawcett, 1961.

DuPlessis, Rachel Blau. *The Pink Guitar: Writing as Feminist Practice*. New York and London: Routledge, 1990.

Dworkin, Andrea. *Right-Wing Women*. New York: Wideview/Perigee Books, 1983.

Eakin, Paul John. *Fictions in Autobiography: Studies in the Art of Self-Invention*. Princeton, N. J.: Princeton University Press, 1985.

Eliot, T. S. "The Waste Land." In *The Complete Poems and Plays, 1909–1950*. San Diego, New York, London: Harcourt Brace Jovanovich, 1952. 37–50.

Felman, Shoshana, and Dori Laub. *Testimony: Crises of Witnessing in Literature, Psychoanalysis, and History*. New York and London: Routledge, 1992.

Ferguson, Russell, et al., eds. *Out There: Marginalization and Contemporary Culture*. Cambridge, Mass. and London, England: MIT Press, 1990.

Fetterly, Judith. *The Resisting Reader: A Feminist Approach to American Fiction*. Bloomington: Indiana University Press, 1978.

Fisher, Dexter, ed. *The Third Woman: Minority Women Writers of the United States*. Boston: Houghton Mifflin, 1980.

Flax, Jane. *Thinking Fragments: Psychoanalysis, Feminism, and Postmodernism in the Contemporary West.* Berkeley and Los Angeles: University of California Press, 1990.

Fox-Genovese, Elizabeth. "To Write My Self: The Autobiographies of Afro-American Women." In Benstock, ed., *Feminist Issues.* 161–80.

Frankenberg, Ruth. *White Women, Race Matters: The Social Construction of Whiteness.* Minneapolis: University of Minnesota Press, 1993.

Freedman, Estelle B., et al., eds. *The Lesbian Issue: Essays from SIGNS.* Chicago: University of Chicago Press, 1985.

Friedman, Susan Stanford. " 'I go where I love': An Intertextual Study of H. D. and Adrienne Rich." In Freedman et al., eds., *Lesbian Issue.* 111–28.

———. "Women's Autobiographical Selves: Theory and Practice." In Benstock, ed., *Feminist Issues.* 34–62.

Frye, Marilyn. *The Politics of Reality: Essays in Feminist Theory.* New York: Crossing Press, 1983.

Fuss, Diana. *Essentially Speaking: Feminism, Nature and Difference.* New York and London: Routledge, 1989.

Gallop, Jane. *The Daughter's Seduction: Feminism and Psychoanalysis.* Ithaca, N. Y.: Cornell University Press, 1982.

———. *Thinking Through the Body.* New York: Columbia University Press, 1988.

———. "*Writing and Sexual Difference*: The Difference Within." In Abel, ed., *Writing.* 283–90.

Gardiner, Judith Kegan. "On Female Identity and Writing by Women." In Abel, ed., *Writing.* 177–92.

Gates, Henry Louis Jr., ed. *"Race," Writing, and Difference.* Chicago: University of Chicago Press, 1986.

Gilbert, Sandra, and Susan Gubar. *The Madwoman in the Attic: The Woman Writer and the Nineteenth Century Literary Imagination.* New Haven, Conn.: Yale University Press, 1979.

——— and ———. "Sexual Linguistics: Gender, Language, Sexuality." *New Literary History* 16.3 (1985): 515–43.

Green, Rayna, ed. *That's What She Said: Contemporary Poetry and Fiction by Native American Women.* Bloomington: Indiana University Press, 1984.

Greene, Gayle, and Coppelia Kahn, eds. *Making a Difference: Feminist Literary Criticism.* London and New York: Methuen, 1985.

Grewal, Inderpal, and Caren Kaplan, eds. *Scattered Hegemonies: Postmodernity and Transnational Feminist Practices.* Minneapolis: University of Minnesota Press, 1994.

Gusdorf, Georges. "Conditions and Limits of Autobiography." In Olney, ed., *Autobiography: Essays.* 28–48.

Haraway, Donna. *Simians, Cyborgs, and Women.* New York and London: Routledge, 1991.

Heath, James and Michael Payne, eds. *Text, Interpretation, Theory.* Lewisburg: Bucknell University Press, 1985.

Heath, Stephen. "Male Feminism." In *Men Is Feminism.* Ed. Alice Jardine and Paul Smith. New York and London: Methuen, 1987. 1–32.

Hinz, Evelyn J. "Mimesis: The Dramatic Lineage of Auto/Biography." In *Essays on Life Writing: From Genre to Critical Practice.* Ed. Marlene Kadar. Toronto: University of Toronto Press, 1992. 195–212.

Homans, Margaret. *Women Writers and Poetic Identity.* Princeton, N. J.: Princeton University Press, 1980.

hooks, bell. *Ain't I a Woman: Black Women and Feminism.* London: Pluto Press, 1981.

———. *Feminist Theory: From Margin to Center.* Boston: South End Press, 1984.

————. *Sisters of the Yam: Black Women and Self-Recovery.* Boston: South End Press, 1993.

————. *Yearning: Race, Gender, and Cultural Politics.* Boston: South End Press, 1990.

Hosek, Chaviva, and Patricia Parker, eds. *Lyric Poetry: Beyond New Criticism.* Ithaca, N. Y.: Cornell University Press, 1985.

Hull, Gloria, Patricia Bell Scott, and Barbara Smith, eds. *All the Women Are White, All the Blacks Are Men, But Some of Us Are Brave: Black Women's Studies.* New York: Feminist Press, 1982.

Irigaray, Luce. *Speculum of the Other Woman.* Trans. Gillian C. Gill. Ithaca, N. Y.: Cornell University Press, 1985.

————. *This Sex Which Is Not One.* Trans. Catherine Porter with Carolyn Burke. Ithaca, N. Y.: Cornell University Press, 1985.

Jack, Ian. "Groups Outraged Over Engineering Incident." *Varsity* October 1, 1987: 1.

Jardine, Alice A. *Gynesis: Configurations of Woman and Modernity.* Ithaca, N. Y.: Cornell University Press, 1985.

Jay, Paul. *Being in the Text.* Ithaca, N. Y.: Cornell University Press, 1984.

Jelinek, Estelle C. *The Tradition of Women's Autobiography: From Antiquity to the Present.* Boston: Twayne, 1986.

———— ed. *Women's Autobiography: Essays in Criticism.* Bloomington: Indiana University Press, 1980.

Johnson, Barbara. *The Critical Difference: Essays in the Contemporary Rhetoric of Reading.* Baltimore: Johns Hopkins University Press, 1980.

Jones, Ann Rosalind. "Inscribing feminity: French theories of the feminine." In Greene and Kahn, eds., *Making a Difference.* 80–112.

————. "Writing the Body: Toward an Understanding of *l'Ecriture Feminine.*" In Showalter, eds., *New Feminist Criticism.* 361–77.

Jordan, June. "The Craft That the Politics Requires: An Interview with June Jordan." By Margaret Kristakos. *Fireweed* 36 (Summer 1992): 26–39.

Juhasz, Suzanne. "Towards a Theory of Form in Feminist Autobiography: Kate Millett's *Flying* and *Sita*; Maxine Hong Kingston's *The Woman Warrior.*" In Jelinek, ed., *Women's Autobiography.* 221–37.

Kalstone, David. *Five Temperaments.* New York: Oxford University Press, 1977.

Kaplan, Caren. "The Politics of Location as Transnational Feminist Critical Practice." In Grewal and Kaplan, eds., *Scattered Hegemonies.* 137–52.

Kaplan, Cora. "Pandora's box: subjectivity, class and sexuality in socialist feminist criticism." In Greene and Kahn, eds., *Making a Difference.* 146–76.

Kennard, Jean E. "Ourself Behind Ourself: A Theory for Lesbian Readers." In Freedman et al., eds., *Lesbian Issue.* 153–68.

Keyes, Claire. *The Aesthetics of Power: The Poetry of Adrienne Rich.* Athens and London: University of Georgia Press, 1986.

Kolodny, Annette. "The Lady's Not for Spurning: Kate Millett and the Critics." In Jelinek, ed., *Women's Autobiography.* 238–59.

Koolish, Lynda. "The Bones of This Body Say, Dance: Self-Empowerment in Contemporary Poetry by Women of Color." *A Gift of Tongues: Critical Challenges in Contemporary American Poetry.* Ed. Marle Harris and Kathleen Aguero. Athens and London: University of Georgia Press, 1987. 1–56.

Kristeva, Julia. *Desire in Language: A Semiotic Approach to Literature and Art.* Trans. Thomas Gora, Alice Jardine, and Leon S. Roudiez. Ed. Leon S. Roudiez. New York: Columbia University Press, 1980.

Kroker, Arthur, and Marilouise Kroker, eds. *Body Invaders: Panic Sex in America.* Montreal: New World Perspectives, 1987.

Lacan, Jacques. *The Four Fundamental Concepts of Psycho-Analysis,* Trans. Alan Sheridan. New York and London: Norton, 1981.

———. *Seminaire II.* Paris: Editions du Seuil, 1978.

———. *Speech and Language in Psychoanalysis.* Trans. Anthony Wilden. Baltimore and London: Johns Hopkins University Press, 1968.

Lorde, Audre. "An Interview With Karla Hammond." *American Poetry Review* March/April 1980: 19.

———. *The Cancer Journals.* San Francisco: Spinsters Ink, 1980.

———. *Our Dead Around Us.* New York: Norton, 1986.

———. *Sister/Outsider: Essays and Speeches.* New York: Crossing Press, 1984.

———. *Zami: A New Spelling of My Name.* New York: Crossing Press, 1983.

MacKinnon, Catharine A. *Feminism Unmodified: Discourses on Life and Law.* Cambridge, Mass.: Harvard University Press, 1987.

Marcus, Jane. "Invincible Mediocrity: The Private Selves of Public Women." In *The Private Self.* Ed. Shari Benstock. Chapel Hill and London: University of North Carolina Press, 1988. 114–46.

Markley, Janice. *A New Tradition? The Poetry of Sylvia Plath, Anne Sexton, and Adrienne Rich.* Frankfurt, Bern, New York: Peter Lang, 1984.

Marks, Elaine, and Isabelle de Courtivron, eds. *New French Feminisms: An Anthology.* New York: Schocken, 1981.

Martin, Wendy. *An American Triptych: Anne Bradstreet, Emily Dickinson, and Adrienne Rich.* Chapel Hill: University of North Carolina Press, 1984.

Meese, Elizabeth. *(Sem)Erotics — Theorizing Lesbian: Writing.* New York: New York University Press, 1992.

Miller, J. Hillis. *The Linguistic Moment: From Wordsworth to Stevens.* Princeton, N. J.: Princeton University Press, 1985.

Miller, Nancy K. "Changing the Subject: Authorship, Writing and the Reader." In de Lauretis, ed., *Feminist Studies/Critical Studies.* 102–20.

———. *Getting Personal: Feminist Occasions and Other Autobiographical Acts.* New York: Routledge. 1991.

Millett, Kate. *The Basement: Meditations on a Human Sacrifice.* New York: Simon and Schuster. 1979.

———. *Flying.* New York: Alfred A. Knopf. 1974.

———. *Sexual Politics.* New York: Ballantine Books, 1969.

———. *Sita.* New York: Ballantine Books, 1977.

Modleski, Tania. *Feminism without Women: Culture and Criticism in a "Postfeminist" Age.* New York and London: Routledge, 1992.

Moi, Toril. *Sexual/Textual Politics: Feminist Literary Theory.* London and New York: Methuen, 1985.

Moraga, Cherríe. "From a Long Line of Vendidas: Chicanas and Feminism." In de Lauretis, ed., *Feminist Studies/Critical Studies.* 173–90.

———. *Loving in the War Years: lo que nunca paso por sus labios.* Boston: South End Press, 1983.

——— and Gloria Anzaldúa, eds. *This Bridge Called My Back: Writings by Radical Women of Color.* Watertown, Mass.: Persephone Press, 1981.

Morgan, Robin. *The Anatomy of Freedom: Feminism, Physics, and Global Politics.* New York: Anchor, 1984.

———, ed. *Sisterhood Is Global: The International Women's Movement Anthology.* New York: Anchor, 1984.

Natoli, Joseph, ed. *Tracing Literary Theory.* Urbana and Chicago: University of Illinois Press, 1987.

Neuman, Shirley. "Autobiography, Bodies, Manhood." In *Prose Studies:* 136–65.

———. "Autobiography: From a Different Poetics to a Poetics of Differences." In *Essays on Life Writing: From Genre to Critical Practice.* Ed. Marlene Kadar. Toronto: University of Toronto Press, 1992. 214–30.

———. "Importing Difference." *A Mazing Space: Writing Canadian Women Writing.* Ed. Shirley Neuman and Smaro Kamboureli. Edmonton: Longspoon/NeWest, 1986. 392–405.

———, ed. *Prose Studies, Special Issue on Autobiography and Questions of Gender.* 14.2 (1991).

Newton, Judith and Deborah Rosenfelt, eds. *Feminist Criticism and Social Change: Sex, Class and Race in Literature and Culture.* New York and London: Methuen, 1985.

O'Neale, Sondra. "Inhibiting Midwives, Usurping Creators: The Struggling Emergence of Black Women in American Fiction." In de Lauretis, ed., *Feminist Studies/Critical Studies* 139–56.

Oates, Joyce Carol. Review of *The Basement: Meditations on a Human Sacrifice* by Kate Millett. *New York Times Book Review* September 9, 1979: 14.

Olney, James, ed. *Autobiography: Essays Theoretical and Critical.* Princeton, N. J.: Princeton University Press, 1980.

———. *Metaphors of Self: The Meaning of Autobiography.* Princeton, N. J.: Princeton University Press, 1972.

———. "Some Versions of Memory/Some Versions of *Bios*: The Ontology of Autobiography." In Olney, ed., *Autobiography: Essays.* 236–67.

———. *Tell Me Africa: An Approach to African Literature.* Princeton: Princeton University Press, 1973.

Ortiz, Simon J., ed. *Earth Power Coming: Short Fiction in Native American Literature.* Tsaile, Ariz.: Navajo Community College Press, 1983.

Ostriker, Alicia Suskin. "Her Cargo: Adrienne Rich and the Common Language." In *Writing Like a Woman.* Ann Arbor: University of Michigan Press, 1983. 102–25.

———. *Stealing the Language: The Emergence of Women's Poetry in America.* Boston: Beacon, 1986.

Penelope, Julia. "Hetropatriarchal Semantics: Just Two Kinds of People in the World." *Lesbian Ethics* 2 (1986): 58–80.

Perreault, Jeanne. "White Feminist Guilt, Abject Scripts, and (Other) Transformative Necessities." *Colour. An Issue.* Ed. Roy Miki and Fred Wah. *West Coast Line* 13/14 (Spring-Fall, 1994): 226–38.

———. "Writing White: Linda Griffiths' Raced Subjectivity in *Jessica.*" (Forthcoming).

Phelan, Peggy. *Unmarked: The Politics of Performance.* London and New York: Routledge, 1993.

Phelan, Shane. *Identity Politics: Lesbian Feminism and the Limits of Community.* Philadelphia: Temple University Press, 1989.

Piercy, Marge. *Parti-Colored Blocks for a Quilt.* Ann Arbor: University of Michigan Press, 1982.

Probyn, Elspeth. *Sexing the Self: Gendered Positions in Cultural Studies.* London and New York: Routledge, 1993.

Przyblowicz, Donna, Nancy Hartsock, and Pamela McCallum, eds. "Introduction: The Construction of Gender and Modes of Social Division I." *Cultural Critique* 13 (1989): 5–14.

Riley, Denise. *"Am I That Name?" Feminism and the Category of "Women" in History*. Minneapolis: University of Minnesota Press, 1988.

Rich, Adrienne. *Blood, Bread, and Poetry: Selected Prose, 1979–1985*. New York: Norton, 1986.

———. "Comment on Friedman's 'I go where I love'; An Intertextual Study of H. D. and Adrienne Rich." In Freedman et al., eds., *Lesbian Issue*. 129–32.

———. *The Dream of a Common Language*. New York: Norton, 1978.

———. *The Fact of a Door Frame*. New York: Norton, 1984.

———. *Of Woman Born: Motherhood as Experience and Institution*. New York: Norton, 1979.

———. *On Lies, Secrets, and Silence: Selected Prose, 1966–1978*. New York: Norton, 1979.

———. "Poetry and Experience: Statement at a Poetry Reading" (1964). *Adrienne Rich's Poetry*. Ed. Barbara Charlesworth Gelpi and Albert Gelpi. New York: Norton, 1975. 89.

———. *Snapshots of a Daughter-in-Law*. New York: Norton, 1967.

———. *Time's Power*. New York: Norton, 1989.

———. *Your Native Land, Your Life*. New York: Norton, 1986.

Riffaterre, Michael. *Semiotics of Poetry*. Bloomington: Indiana University Press. 1978.

Rose, Wendy. "Epilogue (to Lost Copper)." In Green, ed., *That's What She Said*. 209.

———. "Poet Woman's Mitosis: Dividing All the Cells Apart." In Green, ed., *That's What She Said*. 206.

Rowbotham, Sheila, Lynne Segal, and Hilary Wainwright, eds. *Beyond the Fragments: Feminism and the Making of Socialism*. Boston: Alyson, 1979.

Rubenstein, Roberta. *Boundaries of the Self: Gender, Culture, Fiction*. Chicago: University of Illinois, 1987.

Russ, Joanna. *How to Suppress Women's Writing*. Austin: University of Texas Press, 1983.

Ryan, Michael. "Self-Evidence." Review of *Le Pacte Autobiographique* by Philip Lejeune. *Diacritics* (June 1980): 2–16.

Said, Edward. "Reflections on Exile." In *Out There: Marginalization and Contemporary Cultures*. Ed. Russell Ferguson et al. New York: New Museum of Contemporary Art, and Cambridge, Mass.: MIT Press, 1990. 357–66.

———. *The World, the Text, and the Critic*. Cambridge, Mass.: Harvard University Press, 1983.

Scarry, Elaine. *The Body in Pain: The Making and Unmaking of the World*. New York and London: Oxford University Press, 1985.

Schor, Naomi. "This Essentialism Which Is Not One: Coming to Grips with Irigaray." *differences* 1.2 (1989): 38–58.

———. *Reading in Detail: Aethetics and the Feminine*. New York and London: Methuen, 1987.

Schweickart, Patrocinio P., "Towards a Feminist Theory of Reading." In *Gender and Reading: Essays on Readers, Texts, and Contexts*. Ed. Elizabeth A. Flynn and Patrocinio P. Schweickart. Baltimore and London: Johns Hopkins University Press, 1985. 31–62.

Showalter, Elaine, ed. *The New Feminist Criticism: Essays on Women, Literature and Theory*. New York: Pantheon Books, 1985.

Silko, Leslie Marmon. *Storyteller*. New York: Seaver Books, 1981.

Smith, Barbara. "Toward a Black Feminist Criticism." In Hull, Scott, and Smith, eds., *All the Women*. 157–75.

Smith, Paul. *Discerning the Subject*. Minneapolis: University of Minnesota Press, 1988.

Smith, Sidonie. "The Autobiographical Manifesto: Identities, Temporalities, Politics." In Neuman, ed., *Prose Studies*. 186–212.

———. *A Poetics of Women's Autobiography: Marginality and the Fictions of Self-Representation*. Bloomington: Indiana University Press, 1987.

———. "Who's Talking/Who's Talking Back? The Subject of Personal Narrative." *Signs* 18.2 (1993): 392–406.

———, and Julia Watson, eds. *De/Colonizing the Subject: The Politics of Gender in Women's Autobiography.* Minneapolis: University of Minnesota Press, 1992.

Snitow, Ann, Christine Stansell, and Sharon Thompson, eds. *Powers of Desire: The Politics of Sexuality.* New York: Monthly Review Press, 1983.

Spacks, Patricia Meyer. *Gossip.* New York: Alfred A. Knopf, 1985.

Spelman, Elizabeth V. *The Inessential Woman: Problems of Exclusion in Feminist Thought.* London: Women's Press, 1990.

Spivak, Gayatri Chakravorty. *In Other Worlds: Essays in Cultural Politics.* New York and London: Methuen, 1987.

———. "In a Word." Interview with Ellen Rooney. *differences* 1.2 (Summer 1989): 124–56.

Sprinker, Michael. "Fictions of the Self: The End of Autobiography." In Olney, ed., *Autobiography: Essays.* 321–42.

Stanton, Domna C., ed. *The Female Autograph: Theory and Practice of Autobiography from the Tenth to the Twentieth Century.* Chicago: University of Chicago Press, 1984.

———. "Language and Revolution: The Franco-American Dis-Connection." *The Future of Difference.* Ed. Hester Eisenstein and Alice Jardine. New Brunswick, N. J.: Rutgers University Press, 1980. 73–87.

Stimpson, Catherine R. Introduction. In Benstock, ed., *Feminist Issues.* 1–6.

———. "Zero Degree Deviancy: The Lesbian Novel in English." In Abel, ed., *Writing.* 243–59.

Suleiman, Susan Rubin, ed. *The Female Body in Western Culture: Contemporary Perspectives.* Cambridge, Mass.: Harvard University Press, 1986.

Tate, Claudia, ed. *Black Women Writers at Work.* New York: Continuum, 1984.

Templeton, Barbara Alice. "A Feminist Theory of Poetics: Modern Romanticism." Dissertation. University of Tennessee, 1984.

Timerman, Jacobo. *Prisoner without a Name, Cell without a Number.* Trans. Tony Talbot. New York: Vintage Books, 1982.

Treichler, Paula A., Cheris Kramarae, and Beth Stafford, eds. *For Alma Mater: Theory and Practice in Feminist Scholarship.* Urbana and Chicago: University of Illinois Press, 1985.

Trinh T. Minh-ha. "Difference: 'A Special Third World Women Issue.'" *Discourse: Journal for Theoretical Studies in Media and Culture* 8 (1986–87): 11–37.

———. Introduction. *Discourse* 8 (1986–87): 3–9.

———. "Not You/Like You: Post-Colonial Women and the Interlocking Questions of Identity and Difference." In Anzaldúa, ed., *Making Face.* 371–75.

———. *Woman, Native, Other: Writing, Postcoloniality, and Feminism.* Bloomington: Indiana University Press, 1989.

Vendler, Helen. *Part of Nature, Part of Us: Modern American Poets.* Cambridge, Mass., and London, England: Harvard University Press, 1980.

Vienna Tribunal. Dir. Gerry Rogers. Augusta Productions, with NFB. 54 Mullocks St., St. John's, Newfoundland, Canada, A1C 2R8, 1994.

Walker, Alice. *In Search of Our Mothers' Gardens.* New York: Harcourt Brace Jovanovich, 1984.

Williams, Patricia J. *The Alchemy of Race and Rights: Diary of a Law Professor.* Cambridge, Mass., and London, England: Harvard University Press, 1991.

Willis, Susan. *Specifying: Black Women Writing the American Experience.* Madison: The University of Wisconsin Press, 1987.

Woolf, Virginia. "Women and Fiction." In *Women and Writing.* Ed. Michele Barrett. London: Women's Press, 1979. 43–52.

Yaegar, Patricia. *Honey-Mad Women: Emancipatory Strategies in Women's Writing.* New York: Columbia University Press, 1988.

Zimmerman, Bonnie. "The Politics of Transliteration: Lesbian Personal Narratives." In Freedman et al., eds., *Lesbian Issue.* 251–70.

———. "What Has Never Been: An Overview of Lesbian Feminist Criticism." In Greene and Kahn, eds., *Making a Difference.* 177–210.

Index

Jeanne Perreault is associate professor of English at the University of Calgary. She is the coeditor (with Sylvia Vance) of *Writing the Circle: Native Women of Western Canada* (1990), the first anthology of writings by First Nations women in Canada.